Augustine
wayward genius

Augustine
wayward genius

The life of St. Augustine of Hippo

David Bentley-Taylor

Baker Book House   Grand Rapids, Michigan 49506

Printed in the United States of America

CONTENTS

PART 5   411–420   YEARS OF TRIUMPH AND TRAGEDY

PART 6   420–430   THE HUMBLING YEARS

PREFACE

Like many people I first came to appreciate Augustine of Hippo by reading his *Confessions.* In my enthusiasm I then bought two volumes of his letters, but other interests intervened and for thirty years I never opened them. However, during a prolonged period in Java when I was separated from my family it occurred to me to reread the *Confessions* as though Augustine was my guest, asking him to sit down in the empty chair and share with me the riches of his mind. Then five years ago I entered into a more continuous friendship with him, turning at last to his letters and many of his other writings, giving ear also to those who disapproved of him. I discovered he was a more complicated character than I had realised and that deep shadows as well as bright sunshine fell across the long pathway of his life.

I have aimed to tell his story primarily for those who know little about him and may even have confused him with his namesake, Augustine of Canterbury. I must acknowledge my debt to David Wright, one of the Senior Lecturers in Ecclesiastical History at New College in Edinburgh, for his persistent encouragement and kindly help. I also profited greatly from the advice of my daughter-in-law Margie, who scrutinised the manuscript in detail. The task has been a thrilling one. I feel as though I had been in the Himalayas trying to get to the top of Everest.

PART ONE

354–387
THE SEARCHING YEARS

Chapter One

THE SON OF MONICA

The town of Souk Ahras in eastern Algeria, sixty miles inland from the Mediterranean, marks the site of the ancient city of Tagaste where Augustine was born. From its position, facing south on a steep hillside two thousand feet above sea level, it commanded a panorama of wooded hills crowned in some cases by jagged pinnacles of rock. Below the city the land fell steeply to the gorge of the Medjerda River, rearing up dramatically beyond it till higher ridges closed the view. Within this wide amphitheatre, bisected by the river, were many minor hills cut by ravines, clothed with forests, beautified with cornfields. In winter a cowl of snow rested briefly on the mountains; in summer the scene resembled rural Switzerland without its Alpine peaks.

Some three hundred years after Christ's cruxifixion, when North Africa had been Roman for half a millenium, two girls went down one day to fetch wine from the cellar of a house in Tagaste. One of them was ten-year-old Monica, the other a servant carrying a flagon in which the wine was to be taken up to Monica's parents. Monica had the cup for dipping it out of the barrel, but as no one else was down in the cool cellar it occurred to her to have a sip herself. Not liking the taste, she merely touched it with her lips, but next time they were there she tried it again. On each visit to the cellar she grew bolder, till she would hurriedly gulp down several cups before they went up. Nobody knew about it except the servant. Then one day they quarrelled : the older girl lost her temper and called Monica a little drunkard. She was so afraid her parents would find out that she never did it again.

Two years later a marriage was arranged for her. What

else could be done with a girl when there was no school she could attend and no career open to her? Her husband, Patricius, was an undistinguished youth, generous at times but hot tempered and not faithful to his wife. Her family were Catholic Christians, but Patricius was a pagan. Yet she got on well with him and the couple were considered remarkable because they did not quarrel. Monica's friends were often so badly bullied by their husbands that their faces were scarred and bruised. They could not understand how she avoided being battered in the same way. She explained that from the time of her marriage she had regarded Patricius as her master, so she never got angry or resisted him in any way; if his behaviour had been particularly unreasonable, she would wait till he was in a calm mood and then explain herself.

Having moved into Patricius' home she also had his mother to contend with. In a large establishment there was plenty of opportunity for people to speak bitterly of one another, but Monica tried to play the role of peacemaker. Some of the servants, taking advantage of the helpless little newcomer, whispered malicious things about her to their mistress. At first this poisoned relationships, but before long her mother-in-law was so impressed by Monica's patience that she reported the mischief makers to her son. Patricius had them beaten and from that time harmony prevailed.

A boy and a girl were born to the couple and then in A.D. 354, when she was twenty-three and had been married about ten years, Monica gave birth to another boy whom they named Augustine. He was probably her youngest child. Although 'signed with the sign of the cross as I came new from the womb of my mother', he was not baptised. Other women shared in the task of suckling him. In childhood he absorbed Monica's unquestioning faith in Christ, so when he fell ill and seemed in danger of death he begged to be baptised. As he quickly recovered, nothing was done about it; it was felt better for him to commit sins before baptism rather than afterwards. In view of his mother's religious ardour there was tension with Patricius over his upbringing, but for some years it was Monica's influence which prevailed.

When he started at the local school he had to be forced to work, for he much preferred ball games and for this the masters beat him. His first prayers were that he might not be beaten at school but he so revelled in play that he could not escape the cane. His mother tongue was Latin and gradually he began to enjoy Latin literature, but he loathed the drudgery of learning Greek and never became proficient in it. Virgil he liked, Homer he hated. These studies, however, opened his eyes to evils which soon affected his character and by the time he emerged from childhood he had learned sexual indulgence. Excited by what he saw in the theatre and tempted by the immoralities of the deities he read about at school, his deterioration was rapid. Yet Monica's influence was not altogether eclipsed. 'In my small thoughts upon small matters I had come to delight in the truth, I hated to be wrong, had a vigorous memory, was well trained in speech, delighted in friendship, shunned pain, meanness and ignorance.' Before he reached adolescence the tug-of-war between vileness and discipline had started in his heart.

Nowadays the North African coast is divided between Morocco, Algeria, Tunisia and Libya, but in Augustine's time the entire region lay within the Roman Empire. Morocco and western Algeria comprised the province of Mauretania with its capital at Caesarea, now Cherchell. Eastern Algeria and western Tunisia formed the province of Numidia with its capital at Cirta, now Constantine. The rest of Tunisia was united with Libya in the original Roman province of Africa with its capital at Carthage, now a suburb of Tunis. The annexation of these three regions by the European power had taken place step by step after the destruction of Carthage at the conclusion of the Punic Wars in 146 B.C. Thousands of Romans settled in the conquered lands augmented by colonies established by Julius Caesar and the

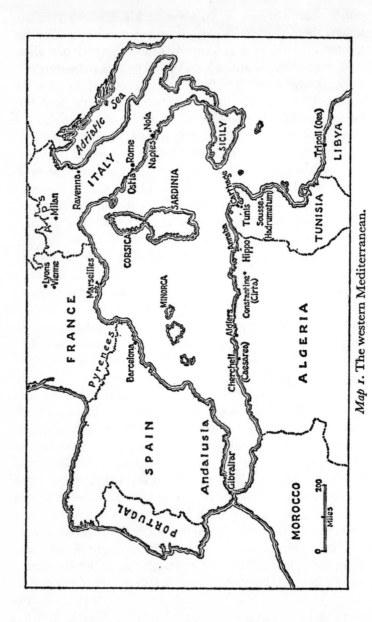

Map 1. The western Mediterranean.

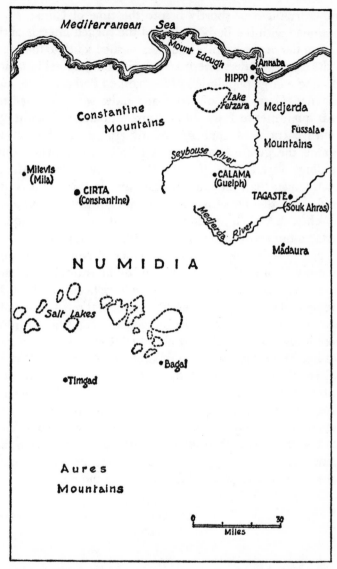

Map 2. Sketch map of the Roman province of Numidia with some modern names added. The town of Annaba did not exist at that time. Many smaller places mentioned by Augustine cannot now be identified.

Emperor Augustus shortly before the time of Christ. War continued with the Berber tribes of the rugged interior until the frontier of the Empire had been pushed south to the edge of the desert. Settlers intermarried with the original inhabitants and a large population of Romanised Berbers came into existence. Corn, olive oil, fruit and hides were exported in great quantities to Italy, while Roman financiers bought up extensive tracts of country and the Emperors themselves became the greatest landowners of all. Impressive public buildings were erected, for the Romans held North Africa much longer than they held Britain and to this day it is littered with the remains of their cities, theatres, temples, churches, baths, hippodromes, amphitheatres and aqueducts : innumerable Roman pillars still reach for the sky.

Tagaste lay in the beautiful province of Numidia, mountainous and primitive, dividing the Mediterranean from the Sahara. It was no great advantage to have been born in such a remote place. As one of the settler population, a wide gulf separated Augustine from the indigenous people, apart from those whose families had long absorbed Roman language and culture. The majority of the inhabitants spoke some Berber dialect of the hinterland or else Punic, which had for centuries prevailed in coastal regions ever since the Phoenicians founded Carthage. By contrast with these simple tribesmen, rough farm-labourers, tradesmen and slaves, Augustine was a sophisticated townsman, not trained to work with his hands but not specially privileged either, a very ordinary Roman youth, except that Monica was his mother.

Chapter Two

THE TEENAGER

When Augustine's primary education had been completed, his parents sent him away to study at Madaura, twenty-five miles further south. To get there he had to cross the Medjerda River and climb the formidable hillside beyond. Then the road led to an undulating plateau three thousand feet above sea level, where Madaura lay on rising ground, its paved streets set at right angles to each other, its crossroads graced with pillars at each corner, its central square beside the theatre magnificently colonnaded. He never revealed any details about his time at Madaura, and before long his parents, sensing his intellectual ability, decided he ought to be given the chance of further education at Carthage. The old Phoenician city had experienced a remarkable resurrection to become one of the largest in the Empire. To send their son to study in the capital of Roman Africa was an expense his family could ill afford and their friends much admired them for pursuing the idea. Monica was keen on it because she was anxious about his moral welfare and felt sure that study would help him to become a true Christian.

In order to get together sufficient money they were compelled to bring him back from Madaura in 370, when he was sixteen, and for a year he lived idly at home. This proved a disaster; intellectually he stood still, morally he ran wild. Always a sociable creature, his strong personality tended to make him the central figure in a group of close friends, but he was not yet able to choose friends wisely. With time on his hands and no clear convictions to restrain him, he plunged into rudderless self-indulgence. 'Love and lust boiled within me and swept my youthful immaturity over the precipice of evil desire, to leave me half-drowned in a whirlpool of abominable sins.' Patricius, influenced at last by his wife, was under instruction in the Christian Church but still only superficially moved by its message. One day he saw Augustine stripped at the public baths and went home in delighted excitement to tell Monica he thought they would soon be grandparents. But she did not want him to marry so young in case it interfered with his studies. Too late she urged him not to sin with women, for it was precisely what he had every intention of doing. Unable to distinguish 'the white light of love from the fog of lust', he let himself go. 'I burned for all the satisfactions of hell and sank to the animal in a succession of dark lusts.' Promiscuity left him wretched and restless, arrogant and depressed. His friends were no help. Ashamed to hear others boasting of exploits viler than his own, he set out to imitate them. In such company as he kept, chastity was contemptible, innocence cowardly, evil was pursued just because it was evil, and Monica was powerless to do anything about it. 'The madness of lust took complete control of me.' Yet the only incident he recorded in detail from that disastrous year was comparatively trivial. Late one night, as he and his friends roamed the streets near his parents' orchard, they noticed a neighbour's pear tree loaded with fruit. Roaring with laughter, they knocked it down and carted off a whole load to throw to the pigs—just for fun.

About the time of this pause in Augustine's education, alarming events destined to affect his life took place in Mauretania. The tragic drama of three Berber brothers—Firmus, Gildo and Mascezel—began. During the years 371–374 Firmus masterminded a revolt against the Romans and captured the western capital of Caesarea. Mascezel supported him but Gildo sided with the authorities. It took the despatch of Rome's greatest general to conquer Firmus, who preferred suicide to capture. Mascezel was spared to become useful to the Empire, but it was Gildo who profited most from the upheaval. The Romans rewarded him for his loyalty by making him Count of Africa, their commander-in-chief. He also came to possess great estates inland and in the years ahead gradually built up his power.

When the money was ready, Augustine left Numidia to study at Carthage. Patricius died shortly afterwards, but he recorded the fact without emotion. However, the loss of his father posed a serious financial threat to his plans, but this was averted by the intervention of Romanianus, a wealthy citizen of Tagaste who had known him from childhood. Long afterwards Augustine revealed the full extent of his help. 'When I was a poor boy, pursuing studies that were not available in our town, you provided me with a home, with funds, and with something better—courage. When I was bereaved of a father, you consoled me with your friendship, roused me with your encouragement, and aided me with your resources. By your favour and friendship you made me almost as renowned and prominent a personage as yourself in our town.'

But once out of Monica's sight he was totally free to continue the vicious way of life on which he had embarked. 'A cauldron of illicit loves leaped and boiled about me.' He deliberately offered his vile deeds to devils and once committed an undefined act of sacrilege in a church. 'What wonder that I became infected with a foul disease?' His passion for the stage only added fuel to his flame. He preferred plays which radically stirred his emotions, 'yet, as if they had been fingernails, their scratching was followed by swelling and inflammation and sores with pus flowing.' In spite of this, his innate ability soon made him a leader in the school of rhetoric. And he became deeply attached to Carthage, set well back in the only large bay on the north coast of Africa with a lake behind it, its harbour and naval base looking across the water to the mountains of Cape Bon, its crowded streets, its huge public baths, its wealthy homes with their beautiful mosaic floors, its colossal amphitheatre where helpless men were pitted against professional gladiators and wild beasts, and its theatre seating twenty thousand people. All his life he found it hard to keep away from Carthage for long.

The curriculum required him to study a book on philosophy by Cicero. 'The one thing that delighted me in Cicero's exhortation was that I should love, seek and embrace not this or that philosophical school but Wisdom itself, whatever it might be. The book excited and inflamed me. In my ardour the only thing I found lacking was that the name of Christ was not there. For with my mother's milk my infant heart had drunk in, and still held deep down in it, that name— and whatever lacked that name, no matter how learned and excellently written and true, could not win me wholly.' This experience drove him to study the Bible for the first time. He had no idea what books it contained but when he began to read them he was repelled by their simplicity. 'They seemed to me unworthy to be compared with the majesty of Cicero.' So he soon gave up.

As a result he had no anchorage for his mind when at the age of eighteen he came across the Manichees, a religious group originating in the previous century in Iran, which combined philosophical speculation and primitive superstition with ideas derived from Judaism and Christianity. 'They declared they would lay aside all authority and by pure and simple reason would bring to God those who were willing to listen to them. What else compelled me to spurn the religion implanted in me as a boy by my parents and to follow these men but that they said we were overawed by superstition and were told to believe rather than to reason, whereas they pressed no one to believe until the truth had been discussed and elucidated? Who would not be enticed by these promises, especially if he were an adolescent with a mind eager for truth but made proud and garrulous by the disputes of learned men at school? Such they found me then, scorning what I took to be old wives' fables and desirous of holding the open and sincere truth which they promised.'

Since Manicheism taught that from the beginning there had been two eternal Principles opposed to one another, God and Satan, it had a ready answer to the problem of evil, feeling no necessity to reconcile its existence with the character of God. Upon this fundamental dualism was grafted a fantastic mythology in which the sun and the moon played their part in the liberation of elements of the kingdom of light imprisoned in the kingdom of darkness. Manicheism was implacably opposed to the Old Testament's representation of God and equally convinced that the text of the New Testament had been corrupted on every page, so it saw no need to defend the Bible against its critics. From its more devoted adherents it demanded an ascetic way of life, including celibacy, but all its disciplines were inextricably entangled in a jungle of myths. Before long Augustine came to believe in a weird assortment of fantasies : in the Five Elements striving with the Five Dens of Darkness; in God as a kind of material resplendence; and in the ability of Manichean saints to digest figs and then, with groaning and prayer, breathe them out as particles of the Godhead. In later life his verdict was 'I let myself be taken in by fools' and he bitterly regretted that for the next nine years 'I lay tossing in the mud of that deep pit'.

At this point Monica moved back into his life. She was now a widow without younger children to care for, so she came to Carthage, though so dismayed at his adoption of Manichean beliefs that at first she refused to eat with him. She was no match for him in argument but that did not stop her praying, dreaming dreams and enlisting the aid of better educated people. As she prayed she wept, pressing her face right down on to the ground. In one of her dreams a radiant youth assured her that one day her son would join her, but Augustine was not impressed when she told him about it. He interpreted the dream to mean that she would join him, but she would have none of it. 'No, for it was not said to me "Where he is, you are", but "Where you are, he is" ', and he never quite forgot that. Fortunately this dream encouraged her to have meals with him again. Then she asked a bishop she knew to talk with the boy and set him on the right path. To her regret he refused, feeling it was useless while Augustine was so enamoured with his new ideas. 'Let him alone', he said, 'only pray to the Lord for him. He will himself discover by reading what his error is.' Then the bishop revealed that he had been brought up as a Manichee but eventually found his own way out of the sect. This only made Monica more sure he was the man to help her. To his dismay she burst into tears and he rather lost patience. 'It is impossible that the son of these tears should perish,' he said. She could not persuade him, but she took his words as God's answer to her.

For the moment the outlook was unpromising. Proud of his attainments, already a teacher of rhetoric applauded for his poetry, obsessed with the theatre, eager to make money, carrying food to the Manichean elect so that 'in the factory of their stomachs they should turn it into angels and deities', and given over to untempered lusts, he was a constant distress to her. Then all of a sudden his sexual promiscuity ceased. 'In those years I took one woman, not joined to me in lawful marriage, but one whom wandering lust and no particular judgment brought my way. Yet I had but that one woman and I was faithful to her. And with her I learnt by my own experience what a gulf there is between the restraint of the marriage covenant entered into for the sake of children and the mere bargain of a lustful love, where if children come they come unwanted—though when they are born they compel our love.' For a child did come, a boy, whom they called Adeodatus. Augustine never even mentioned the girl's name. She was his sin, not his wife. But he no longer ran wild.

Chapter Three

THE LONG ORDEAL

From his nineteenth to his twenty-ninth year Augustine remained in such a state of confusion and perversity that he could only look back upon this period with shame. Meanwhile the western half of the Roman Empire, in which he was living, passed into an equally unhealthy condition. The capable Emperor Valentinian I died when Augustine was twenty-one and for the rest of his life the mantle of imperial responsibility fell upon a succession of infants and boys, guided by their widowed mothers, growing into mediocre young men pathetically lacking the ability to weather the storms which history unleashed upon them. Authority was divided between the Emperor's sons : Gratian, aged sixteen, lived at Trier in Germany; Valentinian II, aged four, lived at Milan in Italy with his mother Justina.

Augustine's mental agility soon enabled him to outstrip his student contemporaries at Carthage. When a professor of rhetoric warmly commended the *Categories*—Aristotle's introductory treatise on logic in which he classifies words according to the kinds, or categories, of objects they signify— he got hold of a copy and easily mastered it, whereas the others could barely make head or tail of it, even with the aid of teachers drawing diagrams in the dust to illustrate their lectures. His sharp mind gravitated to other sharp minds, so he admired Vindicianus, physician to the late Emperor. It happened that Augustine had just entered for a poetic contest and a magician had guaranteed him victory if he made use of his rites and sacrifices. He indignantly refused, won the prize without such aids, and was crowned with a wreath by Vindicianus himself. Attracted by the vitality of the old

man's talk, Augustine spoke to him approvingly of horo-
scope-casters and their books which traced the cause of
human triumphs and disasters to the movements of the planets. 'With much fatherly kindness he advised me to throw
them away and not waste upon such nonsense time and
trouble which could be put to better use.' The occasional
success of stargazers in foretelling the future Vindicianus
attributed to chance, for which he felt allowance should
always be made. Though partially convinced, this conversation did not deflect Augustine from astrological study, even
when the doctor's advice was reinforced by the goodnatured
ridicule of Nebridius, a youth from an estate near Carthage
who became one of his closest friends throughout these years.
Augustine admired Nebridius for his moral restraint, though
he could not imitate it, but at least he had begun to choose
his friends more wisely than before.

After graduating from Carthage he became a schoolmaster
back home at Tagaste. One of his pupils was a boy named
Alypius, a relative of his patron Romanianus. 'He was much
attached to me because he thought me kindly and learned,
and I to him because of the great bent towards virtue that
was so marked in him so young.' Alypius' life was destined
to be intertwined with his own, but for the moment he was
more closely associated with a boy he never named, whom
he had drawn into Manicheism. When this youth became
seriously ill, Augustine would not leave his bedside. As he lay
unconscious and apparently at the point of death, his family
had him baptised, but his fever abated and as soon as they
could talk Augustine poured scorn on what had been done to
him. However, the sick man roused himself and in an un-
expected outburst of independence told Augustine to stop
such talk. It seemed all right to leave, so Augustine withdrew,
but shortly afterwards the boy relapsed and died. To this
Augustine reacted with extraordinary intensity. 'I raged and
sighed and wept and was in torment, unable to rest, unable
to think. I bore my soul all broken and bleeding and loathing

to be borne by me, and I could find nowhere to set it down to rest. Not in shady groves, nor in mirth and music, nor in perfumed gardens, nor in formal banquets, nor in the delights of bedroom and bed, nor in books nor in poetry could it find peace. I hated all things, hated the very light itself.' He became so unhappy in Tagaste that he decided to return to Carthage. Saying nothing to Monica, he talked first to Romanianus. His patron was reluctant for Tagaste to lose him, but finding that he was 'unable to subdue the yearning of a young man striving for what seemed to be better things', he financed the trip.

Back in Carthage Augustine was gradually healed by the passage of time and the company of friends of the type he now preferred. 'All kinds of things rejoiced my soul in their company—to talk and laugh and do each other kindnesses; read pleasant books together; pass from lightest jesting to talk of the deepest things and back again; differ without rancour, as a man might differ with himself, and when most rarely dissension arose find our normal agreement all the sweeter for it; teach each other to learn from each other; be impatient for the return of the absent, and welcome them with joy on their homecoming; these and suchlike things, proceeding from our hearts as we gave affection and received it back, and shown by face, by voice, by the eyes, and a thousand other pleasing ways, kindled a flame which fused our very souls and of many made us one.'

Alypius also moved to Carthage, but did not at first study under his former teacher because of some disagreement between his father and Augustine. 'I took it for granted that he would feel about me as his father did. In fact, he did not. He fell into the way of greeting me when we met and of coming sometimes into my school to listen a while and be off.' To this we owe the most vivid picture we have of Augustine as a schoolmaster. 'One day when I was sitting in my usual place with my students in front of me, Alypius came in, greeted me, sat down, and gave his attention to what was being discussed. I had in hand a passage that I was expounding and it suddenly struck me that it could be very well illustrated by a comparison taken from the Games—a comparison which would make the point I was establishing clearer and more amusing, and which involved biting mockery of those who were slaves to that particular insanity.' By 'the Games' he meant the murderous gladiatorial shows at the amphitheatre. He had completely forgotten that Alypius was passionately devoted to these ghastly spectacles, but the latter presumed he had mentioned them for his special benefit. 'Another might have taken it as a reason for being angry with me, but the youth was honest enough to take it as a reason for being angry with himself and for warmer attachment to me.'

He remained for some years in Carthage. Adeodatus and his mother were there too, though he never bothered to mention them. When he was twenty-six he published two or three books entitled *The Beautiful and the Fitting*. 'I no longer have them; somehow or other they have been lost.' He dedicated them to a Syrian in Rome of whose great learning in philosophy he had heard. He wished to attain such eminence himself, but his throbbing mind still wandered through a Manichean maze of trivial follies. Thinking that he perceived in virtue a certain unity in which lay the nature of truth and the supreme Good, he called this a monad, a mind without sex. In vice he detected a dividedness, 'some substance of irrational mind' which he called a dyad, drifting off into unrealities 'invented by my own folly playing upon matter'. But he was rather impressed when a Christian named Elpidius came to Carthage debating with the Manichees and produced arguments from the Bible which were not easy to answer. Augustine did not think much of the Manichean retort that the New Testament text had been corrupted by unknown persons. When he himself met Christians he could produce his own awkward ideas. 'Like the argumentative fool that I was, I put to them the question, "Why does the soul err if God created it?"'

He did his best to turn Romanianus into a Manichee but privately confessed to him his own inner turmoil. Romanianus also continued to give him financial support, otherwise he would have been 'held back by kinsfolk whose very life depended on my occupation and by various expenses occasioned by the wretched distress of my relatives'. With this encouragement he read fast and wide in philosophy, mathematics, logic, music and astronomy. He was fascinated by the mysterious constellations, the Great Bear, the planets; by solstices, equinoxes and eclipses; by the alternations of night and day; by bird, beast, fish, tree and sand. He became increasingly aware that the principles at which he arrived could not be harmonised with the fables of Manicheism, and he was grieved by the restless wickedness of men — 'all the universe is beautiful about them, but they are vile.' In 383, at the age of twenty-nine, he became professor of rhetoric at Carthage. By then the claim made by Mani, the founder of Manicheism, that the Holy Spirit resided in him personally with plenary authority seemed rather ridiculous.

At that point there arrived in the city a charming and intelligent man whom Augustine had long desired to meet, Faustus, a bishop of the Manichees. Having with some difficulty arranged to have a thorough discussion with him, Augustine began by setting out the mathematical explanations of astronomical phenomena by which he was attracted, and in no time Faustus realised he was hopelessly outclassed. 'He knew that he did not know these things and he was not ashamed to admit it. He was not entirely ignorant of his own ignorance.' Augustine liked him all the more for his honesty and they saw a lot of each other. The bishop was keenly interested in literature, so the young professor became his teacher and guided his reading. 'But all my effort and determination to make progress in the sect simply fell away through my coming to know this man. Thus Faustus, who had been a snare to many, did without his knowledge or will begin to unbind the snare that held me.'

Some incidents of a different kind also helped in this process. One day at a busy crossroads in Carthage he chanced to observe a group of Manichean leaders 'accosting some women with indecent sounds and gestures'. He suffered similar disillusionment when a Manichean holy man, whose discussions he had been attending in the district of the fig-sellers, was beaten up by the family of a girl alleged to be with child by him.

In his profession he was daily tormented by the militancy of the students. 'They break in impudently and like a pack of madmen play havoc with the order which the master has established for the good of his pupils. They commit many outrages, extraordinary stupid acts, deserving the punishment of the law if custom did not protect them. When I was a student I would not have such habits in myself, but when I became a teacher I had to endure them in others.' Hearing that discipline was better in Rome, which also promised a rise in salary, he decided to leave Africa and work in Italy. He did not even wait to inform Romanianus. His chief problem was how to get away from Monica, who was still living with him. Like her son, she did not do things by halves. She not only went to church on Sunday but twice every day as well, though he had to admit that she lived out her faith in kindly help to others. Furthermore, 'I have no words to express the love she had for me.' So when the time came for him to leave, she simply followed him to the coast and literally clung to him, weeping and refusing to go home. 'She loved to have me with her, as is the way of mothers, but far more than most mothers.' With great difficulty he persuaded her to sleep near the ship, then lied to her and got away in the night. 'The wind blew and filled our sails and the shore dropped from our sight. Next morning she was frantic with grief.' But she did not give up.

His stay in Rome was not a success. As soon as he arrived he fell seriously ill in the home of a hospitable Manichee. 'I very nearly went to hell bearing all the weight of deadly sins which I had committed.' This time he did not ask for baptism, having decided that Christian beliefs were degrading.

Alypius had preceded him to Rome, working as assessor to the Chancellor of the Italian Treasury. Augustine admired him for his high moral principles, specially when he refused to comply with the wishes of a powerful senator in spite of bribes and threats. Manicheism was strong in the city and Augustine stayed on with the sect, though in an unhappy frame of mind. 'When I got settled in Italy I deliberated long as to how truth was to be found : an inextricable thicket confronted me.' He continued to conceive of God in physical terms. He also thought evil possessed its own formless bulk. He could not accept the virgin birth of Christ, because he considered that would have defiled Him. Yet his enthusiasm for Manicheism had evaporated and he even tried to dissuade his kindly host from believing in its fables. He came to feel truth must be beyond human knowledge and that it was best to treat everything as doubtful. He made no contact with Christians in Rome, not even with Jerome, the great biblical scholar, who had arrived there not long before.

To get established as a teacher of rhetoric he took pupils at his home and through them began to be known. But this did not last long. While it was true that Rome was free from 'the riotous incursions of blackguardly youngsters', he discovered there were other defects in student life in the eternal city. They would gang up together and refuse to pay their fees, so a professor could soon find himself in dire straits. 'My heart hated them and not with righteous hatred.' Barely a year after reaching Rome he heard that a job was available up north in Milan, with travel expenses paid. Supported by his

Manichean friends, he applied for it and delivered a public oration before the prefect of Rome, an illustrious pagan, who approved of the oration and gave the post to Augustine.

Chapter Four

THE TORMENTED PROFESSOR

'So I came to Milan, to the bishop and devout servant of God, Ambrose, famed among the best men of the whole world.' This was indeed an abrupt change from the company Augustine had kept in Rome. 'That man of God received me as a father and as a bishop welcomed my coming.' Ambrose, his senior by fourteen years, was from a more distinguished family than Augustine. His father had been a Roman official with jurisdiction over wide areas of western Europe. Trained from childhood for leadership in public life, Ambrose soon distinguished himself as a lawyer in Milan. When the Catholic bishop died in 374 he was compelled by popular demand to succeed him. Like many people at the time, he had not been baptised in infancy, so in one week he passed from baptism to the episcopacy and found himself in a position of exceptional influence.

Tragic events had taken place while Augustine was in Rome. The twelve-year-old Emperor Valentinian II and his mother Justina, both living in Milan, ruled Italy and North Africa. But his half-brother Gratian, who from Trier controlled Britain, France and Spain, met with disaster. In 383 Maximus, an army officer in Britain, revolted, crossed the Channel, and gave battle to Gratian near Paris. The Emperor's men deserted him in large numbers, so he fled to Lyons, where the governor murdered him. Maximus was thus triumphant north of the Alps and there was an obvious danger that he might invade Italy. At this desperate juncture Justina turned to Ambrose, begging him to go to Trier and persuade the usurper to stay where he was. In this delicate mission Ambrose was remarkably successful, preserving his country from invasion for the time being.

Augustine never explained how he came to meet the bishop beyond saying, 'I was brought by God to him in order that I should be brought by him to God.' But then he traced the course of their friendship in detail. 'I came to love him, not at first as a teacher of truth, but for his kindness towards me.' He had a professional interest in the way Ambrose preached, so he often stood among the crowds of people packed into the church. 'His words I listened to with the greatest care, his matter I held not worthy of attention.' But before long, 'while I was opening my heart to learn how eloquently he spoke, I came to feel, though only gradually, how truly he spoke'. He found it a great help that when preaching from passages in the Old Testament the bishop stressed not so much the literal meaning as the allegorical and spiritual sense to be deduced from it. Perceiving that in this way a reasonable case could be made out for orthodox Christianity, Augustine decided to break his links with Manicheism. Although his mind continued in turmoil, he derived some comfort from the realisation that he had come back to the place where he originally belonged. 'I shall set my foot upon that step on which my parents placed me as a child, until I clearly find the truth.' For the first time in his life he was regularly exposed to intelligent Christian instruction from a man whose character compelled his admiration. 'Nothing of what he said struck me as false, although I did not as yet know whether what he said was true. I held back my heart from accepting anything.'

Then Monica arrived from Africa, braving stormy seas and the long overland journey, still praying, still bemoaning his waywardness, still confident of ultimate triumph. She saw Ambrose for the first time and venerated him like an angel of God for the influence he already had on Augustine. 'When he saw me, he often broke out in her praises, congratulating me that I had such a mother and not realising what sort of a son she had.' Both at home and in Rome she had been accustomed to fast on Saturdays, but this was not the practice in

Milan, so Monica wondered what to do. She got Augustine to ask Ambrose about it. 'When I am here,' the Bishop replied, 'I do not fast on Saturday, but when I am at Rome, I do.' This completely satisfied her. In Africa she also used to visit the little chapels built in honour of earlier Christian martyrs, going from shrine to shrine with her basket of bread and wine, but she stopped doing so on hearing that Ambrose had forbidden it.

By this time Augustine was eager to have a private talk with the bishop. However, it was not to be. Trained as an administrator rather than a theologian, Ambrose had to keep learning while he taught others, so he combined a certain accessibility with an intensive programme of study. Although visitors were allowed to enter his room, he paid no attention to them but just went ahead with his reading. Several times Augustine and his friends sat there watching him, but Ambrose remained unaware of the unique opportunity presented to him in the awkward young professor whose mother haunted the church. 'The agitation working in me required that he should be fully at leisure if I were to pour it out before him, and I never found him so.' But he heard him every Sunday in church and gradually it dawned upon him that when mankind was said to have been made in the image of God this did not imply that God had the shape of a human body.

Tormented by uncertainty, reluctant to commit himself to any beliefs after his disillusionment with the Manichean fables, not at all attracted by Ambrose's celibacy, yet slowly acquiring some sense of the authority of the Bible, he met with constant disappointments in his search for fame and financial security. 'I was in utter misery.' One day when he was writhing with shame over a flattering speech he had to make in praise of the boy Emperor, he spotted a drunken beggar in the street and envied him his scrap of happiness. He said as much to Alypius and Nebridius, his inseparable friends, who had come on to Milan to be with him. The trio were in equal distress, searching desperately for some solution to their need for understanding and moral power.

Each morning he was teaching. Afternoons and evenings were devoted to preparing his lectures and calling on important people whose help he needed. At times he dreamed that his influential friends might get him a governorship so that he could end his financial worries by marrying an heiress. Adeodatus' mother had accompanied him to Milan but no one regarded him as a married man. Alypius was strongly against him being properly married as he felt they would not then be able to go on living together in the pursuit of wisdom. Monica took the opposite view, hoping that after a respectable marriage he might be baptised. Eventually he did propose to a girl and gained her family's consent. As she was still a minor, he agreed to wait two years. Yet at the same time he exerted such an influence upon his men friends that a group of them seriously considered pooling their financial resources and living together in a philosophers' commune. No one was more enthusiastic about this than Romanianus, who had come over from Tagaste to the imperial court on business. His great wealth made the scheme attractive to the others but since some of them were married the whole plan eventually fell through. Then 'she with whom I had lived so long was torn from my side as a hindrance to my forthcoming marriage : she went back to Africa, swearing she would never know another man'. Both of them were heartbroken, for in its way the alliance had not been unsuccessful. Adeodatus, a teenager by this time, remained with his father. However, the two-year wait proved intolerable to Augustine : in bitter grief he took another mistress, but without diminishing his misery. 'Because my will was perverse, it changed to lust, and lust yielded to became habit, and habit not resisted became necessity.'

Then a tremendous struggle broke out in Milan between the Catholic Church and Justina, the young Emperor's mother. She had little love for Ambrose since she belonged to the Arian party which had caused much dissension by its denial of the deity of Christ. Justina demanded that the main church in the city be handed over to the Arians and she moved up troops to enforce her wishes. Although the building was ringed by soldiers, the Catholics stayed there day and night to preserve it, singing psalms and hymns to keep their spirits up. Monica felt totally involved in the crisis and even Augustine, though so distracted by his own mental muddle and moral wretchedness, was excited at the disturbed state of the city. Enough of his Christian inheritance remained in his mind for him to be sure death was not the end of everything, but he feared he might die before he found the truth. Along with Alypius and Nebridius he was particularly depressed by their vain search for an alternative to the Manichean explanation of the existence of evil. Instead of attributing it to the very nature of things, to an eternally existing force, he began to weigh the suggestion that it is our own free will which causes us to do evil. But then he was dismayed by an answering train of thought. 'Who made me? Was it not my God, who is not only good but goodness itself? What root reason is there for my willing evil and failing to will good, since I was wholly made by my most loving God? If the devil is the author, where does the devil come from? If by his own perverse will he was turned from a good angel into a devil, what was the origin in him of that perverse will, since by the all-good Creator he was made wholly angel?'

He faced the fact that his sinful youth was over and he was now a mature man, 'though so poor a man'. But then his inveterate tendency to think of both God and evil as substances was challenged when he came across the books of Plotinus, the Neo-Platonist philosopher, translated from Greek into Latin by Victorinus, formerly professor of rhetoric at Rome. As he studied them, the tumult raging in his mind was somewhat calmed. He began to reason that evil does not really exist at all. 'There are some things which we call evil because they do not harmonise with other things.

35

Yet these same things do harmonise with still others. In themselves they are good. There is no sanity in those whom anything in creation displeases.' On this basis he tried to settle into the conviction that evil had no independent existence and was merely 'a swerving of the will'. But in his unstable condition the insight was fleeting. He felt he had seen there was something to see, yet realised he was not yet the man to see it, though 'I talked away as if I knew a great deal'. Helped to a limited extent by Plotinus, he at last turned to the Epistles of Paul. 'In that pure eloquence I saw One Face and I learned to rejoice with trembling.' Previously he had thought of Christ as a man of marvellous wisdom, but now he was profoundly impressed with the difference between the Platonists and the Scriptures. 'It is one thing to see the land of peace from a wooded mountain-top, yet not find the way to it and struggle hopelessly far from the way with hosts of those fugitive deserters from God, under their leader the Lion and the Dragon, besetting us about and ever lying in wait, and quite another to hold to the way that leads there, a way guarded by the care of our heavenly General.'

He badly needed to talk to someone who had time to listen and skill to counsel him. Ambrose was obviously too busy but it occurred to him to try Simplicianus, an older man of wide experience whose special talent it was to help those more gifted than himself. 'I told him all the wanderings of my error.' Simplicianus heard him through patiently, but when Augustine mentioned Victorinus' translations the old man interrupted him with the story of how this famous pagan scholar had boldly confessed Christ as his master before he died. Augustine longed to imitate him, but he could not. 'The enemy held my will.' So the interview seemed to have been in vain. The three friends went on living together, Monica keeping house for them. Alypius completed his third term as assessor to the Chancellor and planned in future to sell his legal advice to private clients, just as Augustine sold skill in speaking. They had persuaded Nebridius to join the staff of Verecundus, a schoolmaster in Milan and 'a great friend of us all'. Then one day in August 386, when it chanced that Nebridius was out, a visitor called at the house.

Chapter Five

THE TRANSFORMATION

The visitor was Ponticianus, a man from Africa who held an important position at the imperial court in Milan. As they sat talking he chanced to pick up the copy of Paul's Epistles which Augustine had been reading. He was both surprised and pleased to find such a book lying on the table, and he went on to talk about the Egyptian hermit Anthony, of whom neither Augustine nor Alypius had ever heard. Amazed at their ignorance, he launched into a fuller description of monastic communities not only in the deserts of Egypt but close to Milan itself. As the two men gazed at him in silence he went on to tell the story of two state officials who came across a biography of Anthony and were so impressed that they immediately abandoned their jobs in order to serve God alone. Their fiancées also gave up the idea of marriage, dedicating themselves to God instead.

Ponticianus left without appreciating the effect his words had had upon Augustine. 'I stood naked in my own sight.' Comparing his own long hesitation with the quick response of the men whose story he had just heard, he perceived how twisted and unclean he was, how deeply infected with the disease of lust. Such a dreadful sense of shame and sorrow filled his heart that he had to get away from Alypius. He went out into the garden, but Alypius was so alarmed that he followed him. 'There I was, going mad on my way to sanity.' He became so frantic, tortured by the thought of his mistresses, that he again moved away from Alypius and threw himself down weeping under a fig tree at the bottom of the garden. As he lay there in intense distress he heard what seemed to be a child's voice from one of the other houses, saying 'Take and read' over and over again. He rose and went back to where Alypius was sitting, for he had left the copy of Paul's Epistles there. 'I snatched it up, opened it, and in silence read the passage on which my eyes first fell.' It was Romans 13 :13–14, 'Not in orgies and drunkenness, not in sexual immorality and debauchery, not in dissension and jealousy. Rather, clothe yourselves with the Lord Jesus Christ and do not think about how to gratify the desires of the sinful nature.' There was no need for him to read on. 'In that instant, with the very ending of the sentence it was as though a light of utter confidence shone in my heart and all the darkness of uncertainty vanished.' Closing the book, he told Alypius what had happened. Alypius asked to see the verse and read the next one, Romans 14 :1, 'Accept him whose faith is weak', which he applied to himself, sharing in his own way in his friend's experience. There and then the wayward, proud, immoral Augustine, unhappy and full of doubts, was gone. A new Augustine was born 'in that instant'.

The first act of his Christian life could hardly have been bettered. 'We went in to my mother and told her, to her great joy. We related how it had come about. She was filled with triumphant exultation.' The impossible miracle had actually happened : the professor had found his Master. 'I bowed my neck to Your easy yoke and my shoulders to Your light burden, Christ Jesus, my helper and my redeemer. I talked with You as friends talk, my glory, my riches, my salvation, my Lord God.' A conversion had taken place which many have ranked second to that of the Apostle Paul in its significance for the influence of Christianity in the history of mankind.

His immediate concern was to resign from the teaching profession, but he decided it would not be right to do so before the long vacation, due to start in three weeks. Then he was only too relieved to stop lecturing, as he had begun to suffer from chest pains and difficulty in breathing. As soon as term ended he went off to a country house at Cassiciacum lent to him by Verecundus, the schoolmaster with whom

Nebridius worked. Seven other men shared this extended holiday from the autumn of 386 to the spring of 387: his brother Navigius and Alypius; his pupils, Trygetius and Licentius, known as 'the boys'; Lastidianus and Rusticus, 'relatives of mine whom I did not wish to be absent, though they are not trained even in grammar, since I believed their common sense was needed'; and Adeodatus, 'the youngest of all, who promises great success, unless my love deceives me'. All of them were from Africa. Licentius, the son of Romanianus, was passionately devoted to poetry and quite capable of leaving in the middle of a meal to compose verses. 'My mother was also with us, a woman in sex, with the faith of a man, the serenity of great age, the love of a mother, the piety of a Christian.' She played a full part in some of their discussions, which were held in the bathhouse when the weather was inclement. 'Very well expressed,' he commented with a smile after one of her remarks, 'No better answer to my question could have been expected.' Once when she joined the group late and asked how their debate was going, he insisted in spite of her protests that her presence and her question should be recorded by the secretaries who were always with them. At other times she had to stop the talk and push the men in to meals.

They were well served by farm hands, kitchen helpers, and a boy who used to run and call them when food was ready. Weather permitting, they strolled in the fields or sat under the shade of a tree. When their discussions went on after sunset, lamps were brought out to make sure the secretaries missed nothing. But there was plenty of fun and laughter as well as serious talk.

During this breathing space at Cassiciacum Augustine began to write books, though he was such a novice in Christian matters that they were more philosophical than biblical. Indeed Alypius at first maintained that the quality of his writing would be impaired if he so much as mentioned Jesus Christ. Augustine's mind needed time to catch up with his heart. Having for so long been what he called 'a blind, raging snarler against the Scriptures', he was not accustomed to uttering Christian statements, but he learnt rapidly as he meditated with delight on the Psalms. Then this was rudely interrupted by an attack of toothache which became so agonising that he could not even speak. He wrote down an urgent appeal to the others to pray for him and 'as soon as we had gone on our knees in all simplicity, the pain went'.

On his thirty-second birthday, 'after a breakfast light enough not to impede our powers of thinking', he called them together for discussions which continued for three days and were incorporated in *The Happy Life*, the first of all the books he wrote as a Christian to be completed. At one point he threw out the question, 'Who really possesses God?' Little Trygetius, never at a loss for words, blurted out, 'He who does what God wills to be done,' and the rustic relatives agreed. Licentius preferred, 'He who lives an upright life,' while Adeodatus suggested, 'He who has a spirit free from uncleanness.' Monica approved all these opinions, specially the last one. Adeodatus explained that he meant 'one who lives chastely' and, when this too was challenged, added 'how can someone be chaste who refrains only from illicit intercourse but does not desist from a steady pollution of the soul from other sins?' He insisted that 'He is truly chaste who keeps God in mind and devotes himself to Him alone'. Augustine made sure the secretaries got that down.

During the winter months at Cassiciacum he often lay thinking late into the night or in the pre-dawn hours. On one of these occasions he was listening to water as it ran through wooden channels behind the bathhouse, when Licentius made a movement which showed that he was awake and also disturbed some mice. Trygetius proved to be awake as well, so they talked till dawn began to steal in through the windows, discussing 'how it is that, though God has a care for human affairs, perversity is so serious'. It bothered them that fleas are marvellously made, yet human life is in such disorder. Excited by what Augustine was saying, Licentius leapt out of bed and stood over Trygetius demanding, 'I am asking you now, "Is God just?"' Trygetius was too sleepy or too surprised to answer, so Licentius lay down again complaining that the matter had not been satisfactorily explained.

When daylight came the boys got up and 'I, shedding tears, spent some time in prayer', but he was disturbed by Licentius singing Psalm 80 : 7 with gusto — 'Restore us, O God Almighty; make Your face shine upon us, that we may be saved.' The previous evening Monica had reproved him for singing it over and over again in the toilet. 'He chanted it a little more loudly than our mother could bear such words to be repeatedly chanted in that place.'

They had their daily time of prayer together and were moving to the bathhouse to continue discussion when they stopped to watch two cocks fighting in front of the door. This provoked the question, 'Why do all cocks behave in this way?' Augustine took the rest of the day quietly on account of chest pains, though as usual he managed to work through half a book of Virgil with the boys before the evening meal.

Soliloquies, the last of the books he wrote at Cassiciacum, 'in which I question and answer myself about those truths I was specially eager to know, as if there were two of us — Reason and I — whereas I was by myself', began with a prayer which epitomised the change that was coming over his outlook. 'Hear, O hear me, my God, my Lord, my King. Hear me my Father, my Hope, my Wealth, my Honour, my Home, my Salvation, my Light, my Life, hear, O hear me.' God and the Bible had begun to compete with Virgil, Cicero and the philosophers for the control of his mind during that carefree withdrawal from responsibilities and duties in society which he fondly anticipated would be normal for his new way of life.

In preparation for their forthcoming baptism, Augustine wrote to Ambrose asking which part of the Bible he ought to be studying. 'He told me to read Isaiah the prophet, I imagine because he more clearly foretells the calling of the Gentiles than the other Old Testament writers; but I did not understand the first part of his book and, thinking it would be all of the same kind, put it aside, meaning to return to it when I should be more practised in the Lord's way of speech.' So once again Ambrose, who had greatly helped Augustine by his preaching, proved unable to give him the personal counsel he needed. Temperamentally they were very different. The great man who had lived such a steady Christian life from his youth was not quite at his best in dealing with a professor whose background was so different. This did not deter him from baptising Augustine and Alypius by three-fold immersion in the name of the Father, the Son and the Holy Spirit at Easter 387. 'We also took with us the boy Adeodatus, carnally begotten by me in sin. He was barely fifteen, yet he was more intelligent than many a grave and learned man. In this I am but acknowledging to You Your own gifts, O Lord my God, Creator of all and powerful to reshape our shapelessness : for I had no part in that boy but the sin. That he had been brought up by us in Your way was because You had inspired us, no other. We took him along with us, the same age as ourselves in Your grace, to be brought up in Your discipline, and we were baptised and all anxiety as to our past fled away.'

Chapter Six

THE DEATH OF MONICA

After his baptism Augustine, free from teaching rhetoric, continued in Milan the life of study, prayer and discussion which he had established at Cassiciacum. Never again did he refer either to his second mistress or to his child fiancée. He repeatedly tried his hand as an author, not always with success : one book he eventually lost; with another he was not satisfied; of a third he later said, 'It is so obscure that even my own attention flags as I read it.'

Meanwhile the western half of the Roman Empire was again in great danger. When it became evident that Maximus might at any moment launch an invasion of Italy across the Alps, Justina turned once more to Ambrose for help. At her request he went a second time to Trier to confer with the challenger, but he was not even granted an interview and had to return disconsolate after some tense days. The outcome was that in the autumn of 387 Maximus moved his troops skilfully through the mountains and Italy fell to him without a major battle. Justina and Valentinian II succeeded in escaping and put themselves under the protection of Theodosius, Emperor at Constantinople. Although the invader was favourable to Catholic Christianity, Ambrose deemed it expedient to withdraw from Milan on his approach. When several other cities were roughly handled, the bishop went to great lengths to ransom those taken prisoner, selling valuable possessions of the Church to raise the money.

During these anxious days Augustine's company was re-inforced by another young man from Tagaste, a civil servant named Evodius, who had given up his job since his conversion and baptism. To some extent Evodius took the place of

Nebridius, who had missed the crucial interview with Ponticianus as well as the months at Cassiciacum. 'We kept together, meaning to live together in our devout purpose. We
thought deeply as to the place where we might serve God
most usefully. As a result we started back for Africa.'

Augustine did not explain in detail the reasons for this
momentous decision. Italy was, of course, in considerable
turmoil, with Justina planning a comeback supported by
Theodosius. Monica naturally wanted to get home and eventually to be buried alongside her husband. And the whole
group were united by their African origin as well as their
Christian faith. Their roots were not in Europe : indeed all
of them probably had Berbers among their ancestors. Furthermore, Augustine had had a good chance to observe
Ambrose : his heavy duties as minister of a large city church;
his many sermons and innumerable visitors; his lack of
privacy for study and prayer; the alarming persecution to
which he had been subjected; and his involvement in secular
affairs. This was a far cry from the pattern of life he had so
much enjoyed since resigning his professorship and he had no
intention of getting similarly entangled in administrative or
political matters. He was much more attracted by the ways of
the hermit Anthony and the monasteries in the Egyptian
desert, news of which had played such a vital part in his
conversion.

So they left Milan and travelled over the wide Apennine
Mountains and down to Rome, a trip of some three hundred
miles. Then they moved out to Ostia, the old port at the
mouth of the Tiber, ready to embark for Carthage. As before,
Monica was the only woman in the party. Of the rest 'she
took as much care as if she had been the mother of us all and
served us as if she had been the daughter of us all'. Though
she was only fifty-six, this was a considerable age for a
woman at that time and they thought of her as elderly.

One day 'she and I stood leaning in a window which
looked inwards to the garden within the house where we were

staying at Ostia; for there we were away from everybody, resting for the sea voyage from the weariness of our long journey by land. There we talked together, she and I alone, in deep joy'. Describing the occasion long afterwards, Augustine recalled that they discussed what the eternal life of Christians would be like in heaven, in 'that region of richness unending where God feeds Israel forever with the food of truth, where life *is* that Wisdom by which all things are made. And while we were thus talking of His Wisdom and panting for it, with all the effort of our heart we for one instant touched it, then sighing and leaving the first fruits of our spirit bound to it, we returned to the sound of our own tongue. So we said : If to any man the tumult of the flesh grew silent, silent the images of earth and sea and air, and if the heavens grew silent and the very soul grew silent and by not thinking of self mounted beyond self, if all dreams grew silent and every tongue, and in their silence He alone spoke to us, so that we should hear His word, hear Himself—just as we two had in a flash of the mind touched the eternal Wisdom—and if this could continue and so ravish and wrap the beholder in inward joys that his life should eternally be such as that one moment of understanding, would not this be "Enter into the joy of your master" (Matthew 25:21)?'

He did the talking, but Monica shared it all with him and then she said, 'Son, for my own part I no longer find joy in anything in this world. What I am still to do here and why I am here, I know not.' Now that he was a Catholic Christian she felt her life's work was finished.

Barely a week later, while they still waited at Ostia, she became ill. Soon afterwards she said to Navigius and Augustine, 'Here you will bury your mother.' They were surprised that she did not seem concerned at the prospect of dying so far from Tagaste. 'Nothing is far from God,' she said, 'and I have no fear that He will not know at the end of the world from what place He is to raise me up.' As Augustine was looking after her she suddenly remarked what a loving and dutiful son he had been, saying that he had never spoken harshly to her. 'But what possible comparison was there between the honour I showed her and the service she had rendered me?'

On the ninth day of her illness, while they were all standing round her bed, she died. Adeodatus burst into tears but Augustine checked him and thereby restrained his own. Evodius started to chant Psalm 101 and they all joined in. As friends came round to the house Augustine found relief in talking to them while arrangements for the funeral went ahead. At the graveside he did not weep, not even during the final prayers while her body lay by the open grave. When all was over he had a bath and then went fast asleep. On waking he lay in bed repeating the verses of an evening hymn Ambrose had written. And then at last he did what he had stopped Adeodatus doing. 'I found solace in weeping both about her and for her, about myself and for myself. I no longer tried to check my tears, but let them flow as they would, making them a pillow for my heart, and it rested upon them.' He thought no one would blame him that for a while 'I wept for my mother, now dead and departed from my sight, who had wept so many years for me that I should live for ever in God's sight.'

With Monica's passing the long introductory stage of Augustine's life was over.

PART TWO

387–396

YEARS OF READJUSTMENT AND PREPARATION

Chapter Seven

PAUSE AT TAGASTE

As Maximus' fleet was lying offshore, Augustine's party had to return to Rome for the time being. He continued the habit of writing which he had by this time formed. Having been for so long hoodwinked by the Manicheans he wanted to refute their teaching and expose the moral weakness to which he felt it led, for he was impressed by the different standard of behaviour he found among responsible Catholics. On the other hand he was not attracted by what he saw of the life of bishops and priests in Rome. Pestered as they were by such crowds of needy people, he considered it was impossible for them to live a truly holy life or enjoy the kind of inward tranquillity which he had come to value so highly. He had no intention of getting involved in that way himself. What fascinated him were the communities of celibate men, holding everything in common, supporting themselves by manual labour, giving all they could to the poor, and passing their time in prayer, reading, and spiritual conference. He had glimpsed this way of living while he was still in Milan and he now found similar institutions for widows and unmarried girls, who gained their livelihood by spinning and weaving. For the moment he just watched what was going on, taking no prominent part in the work of the Church in Rome and making no lasting friendships there. He was only in transit to Africa.

News reached him that Verecundus, owner of Cassiciacum, had died. Although his wife had long been a Christian, he himself had remained uncommitted. Indeed, so impressed had he been by the emphasis on celibacy which characterised Augustine's conversion, that he regarded his wife as a great hindrance to faith. However, when he fell seriously ill he changed his mind and was baptised.

For the time being Nebridius continued in Milan. 'I read your letter beside my lamp after supper,' Augustine wrote to him, anxious to preserve their close friendship, 'after which I lay down, but not for sleep, for on my bed I meditated and talked thus with myself, Augustine addressing and answering Augustine, "Is it not true, as Nebridius affirms, that I am happy?"' But he could not be bothered with some of Nebridius' questions. 'Why is the world the size it is? I do not know. Its dimensions are what they are and I can go no further. Again, why is the world in the place it now occupies? Here too, it is better not to put the question.' Then he prayed and fell asleep.

During 388 the Emperor Theodosius launched a counter-attack on the West. Maximus was killed and Justina's power restored. In the course of these events Augustine and his friends slipped across to Africa. He had been five years away and was so pleased to be back that he never left his homeland again. He found he had not been entirely forgotten in Carthage. He came across a former student of his named Eulogius, who had meanwhile himself become a teacher. He told Augustine that one evening he had been greatly troubled by his inability to understand a passage of Cicero which he was to expound next morning, but in the night he had a dream in which Augustine appeared to him and explained it all.

Along with Alypius he stayed for a while in the home of a prominent man named Innocentius, who had recently suffered dreadfully in an operation for fistulas in the rectum. Medical treatment had continued but eventually his doctor confessed that one ulcer was inaccessible without a further operation. The patient was so terrified that a consultant from Alexandria was brought in, but he agreed that a fresh incision must be made. Sympathetic visitors came every evening, including a bishop and a deacon named Aurelius who was soon to become bishop of Carthage. The night before the operation Innocentius was so unnerved that he invited them all to return in the morning to be present at his death. They did their best to reassure him, urging him to trust in the Lord, and then they prayed together. 'When we knelt down in the usual way and bent towards the ground, Innocentius hurled himself forward as if someone had pushed him flat on his face and began to pray. It is beyond the power of words to express the manner of his prayer, his passion, his agitation, his flood of tears, his groans, and the sobs which shook his whole frame and almost stifled his breath. Whether the others were praying, whether they could take their attention from him, I could not tell. For my part I was utterly unable to utter a prayer. All I could do was to say this brief sentence in my heart, "Lord, what prayers of Your people do You hear, if You do not hear these?" We rose from our knees and after receiving the bishop's blessing we left, the sick man entreating his visitors to come back in the morning. They arrived as they had promised. The surgeons entered. All preparations had been made which that fateful hour demanded. The fearful instruments were produced, while we all sat there in dumbfounded suspense. While his body was being laid in position, the visitors whose authority was greatest tried to raise the patient's drooping spirits with words of encouragement. The bandages were untied and the place was bared. The surgeon examined it, knife in hand, ready for the incision.' But it was not necessary. Their prayers had been answered. They rejoiced and wept together as they gave thanks to God.

Thus encouraged the group went on to Tagaste and settled down at Augustine's old home to a community life in which all their possessions were shared. Possidius, a youth who joined them at that time, remembered that 'he persevered there for nearly three years, living for God in fasting, prayer and good works, meditating day and night on the laws of the Lord, and imparting to others what God revealed to him during contemplation and prayer'. Such intensive Bible study took the place of formal theological training, while in leading the group he gained experience as a preacher. Such was the impression he made on others that whenever he appeared to be at leisure people would take the opportunity of asking him about any matter that was perplexing them, such as 'Is God the creator of evil?', 'Is fear a sin?', or 'Why did the Son of God appear as a man and the Holy Spirit as a dove?' From time to time he dictated answers to eighty-three such questions which were eventually collected into a book. These three years began to change him from being an intellectual acquainted with secular literature into a Christian teacher characterised by phenomenal knowledge of the Bible. But meanwhile trouble was brewing in the province of Numidia. A generation had passed since Gildo helped the Romans put down his brother's rebellion but at heart he was just as antagonistic to Roman rule. As Count of Africa he was the most powerful man in the land and his ultimate intentions were becoming more obvious.

Nebridius had also returned from Italy and was living at his family home near Carthage. They corresponded frequently in the casual way born of long friendship. Nebridius got the impression that the citizens of Tagaste were making such heavy demands on Augustine that he was being distracted from his primary concerns of study and prayer. He was surprised Romanianus did not restrain them and he half hoped Augustine would decide to move over to his place. He carefully preserved all Augustine's letters, hearing in them 'the voice of Christ and the teaching of Plato and Plotinus'. Then he became ill and in his depression was inclined to blame Augustine for not arranging for them to live together again. 'I am wholly at a loss, my dear Nebridius, what to do with you,' Augustine replied. He even considered having the sick man carried to Tagaste but his mother's possessiveness seemed to rule that out. He thought of commuting back and forth, only to abandon the idea in view of his increasing obligations to his colleagues. To compensate for their prolonged separation Nebridius bombarded him with letters asking his opinion about dreams, memory, the imagination and astronomy, till Augustine had to insist he add no more. Most of these questions lay outside his new interests but in the long winter nights 'not entirely spent in sleep by me', he made a token response, dismissing some matters as too trivial and time absorbing, since 'I have not as much leisure as you imagine'. However, he did grapple briefly with the apparent contradiction between the incarnation of the Son of God and what he neatly called the doctrine of the inseparability of the Persons of the Trinity.

'Nothing is done by the Father which is not also done by the Son and by the Holy Spirit,' he assured Nebridius. 'And nothing is done by the Holy Spirit which is not also done by the Father and by the Son, and nothing is done by the Son which is not also done by the Father and by the Holy Spirit.' He suggested that it is on account of our human weakness that the acts of the Persons of the Trinity are presented in a manner which distinguishes these Persons from one another.

To Augustine's great regret Nebridius did not recover. 'And now he lives in Abraham's bosom. Whatever is meant by that bosom, there my Nebridius lives, my most beloved friend, in the place of which he asked me, a poor ignorant creature, so many questions.'

About the same time, in the year 390, Augustine suffered a still more grievous loss. Every reference in his writings to Adeodatus shows the affection and admiration he had for his son. While they were at Tagaste he produced *The Teacher*, a booklet in the form of a dialogue between the two of them, which gives a delightful impression of the boy's relationship with his father. When Augustine apologised to him for sharpening their minds by indulging in verbal play after the Socratic manner, Adeodatus replied, 'Go on as you have begun, for I shall never consider unworthy of attention anything you may think it necessary to say or do.' He also managed to correct Augustine on the precise meaning of a

Punic word. 'All the ideas which are put into the mouth of the other party to the dialogue were truly his, though he was but sixteen,' Augustine explained long after. 'I had experience of many other remarkable qualities in him. His great intelligence filled me with a kind of awe, and who but God could have been the maker of things so wonderful? But You took him early from this earth and I think of him utterly without anxiety, for there is nothing in his boyhood or youth, or anywhere in him, to cause me to fear.'

And that is all we shall ever know about the fate of Adeodatus, for Augustine never referred to him again.

Chapter Eight

THE END OF A DREAM

Many people in Numidia had an eye on the community of dedicated men at Tagaste. Their leader's dynamic personality, reputation for learning and ability as a writer were widely known. So Augustine took care to avoid going to towns which had no bishop. He had not forgotten the way Ambrose had been forced into a position of responsibility in Church and state. Not being one who enjoyed travelling, he was content to stay where he was unless some very good reason presented itself.

Early in 391, when he was thirty-seven years old, it did seem desirable that he should go to the port of Hippo. Somebody there was anxious to meet him in the belief that if only he could hear the word of God from Augustine he would be able to give up his job and become a full-time Christian. The Church at Hippo already had a highly respected leader in Bishop Valerius, so there were no good grounds for keeping away from it, and in any case Augustine was on the look out for a more suitable location for his group than remote Tagaste. So he set off on horseback for the sixty mile journey over the hill behind the city, down through the woods which blanketed the long ridges descending towards the coast, and across the plain to Hippo.

His talks with the man he had come to see were not successful, as the latter kept deferring the decision at which he had hinted. When Sunday came round, Augustine went to church to hear the bishop preach. He was rather more conspicuous than he had expected. Valerius, only too well aware of his presence, seized the opportunity to tell the people there was urgent need for a second ordained man in Hippo. At once the congregation laid hands on Augustine and brought him to the front amid general acclamation. There was no escape : he was caught, just as Ambrose had been, and ordained on the spot. In the emotion of the moment he could not restrain his tears. Some thought this was because he had not been made a bishop right away, but the real reason was that he knew ordination meant the end of his dream of a tranquil Christian life, withdrawn from the pressures and strife of the world.

When it was all over he frankly told Valerius he was a mere beginner in Christian matters whose past life had not prepared him for the kind of role into which he had suddenly been thrust. 'I did not at any earlier period know how great was my unfitness for the arduous work which now disquiets and crushes my spirit. You think me qualified, whilst I know myself better. I unreservedly believe the doctrines pertaining to our salvation, but my difficulty is how to use this truth for the salvation of others.' He begged to be allowed a short time for prayer and preparation. This was granted in spite of the fears of some people that he might yet elude them.

And so it came about that Augustine moved permanently to Hippo on the Mediterranean, lying between hills at the mouth of the Seybouse River with a three thousand foot mountain immediately to the north. It was not a town to be compared with Carthage, Rome, or Milan, but it was at least less insignificant than Tagaste, which from that time dropped out of his story. In succeeding ages he was to be remembered as 'Augustine of Hippo'.

Bishop Valerius was a mild man, admired by all who have left any account of him. Well aware of his own limited gifts, he was delighted to have Augustine alongside him. Free from envy, he was only too ready to give full scope to the younger man. In those days Christianity was in the ascendant. From its obscure origins in the Middle East it had grown steadily in Mediterranean lands, surviving a series of imperial persecutions. Then came its most severe test, the fiercer persecu-

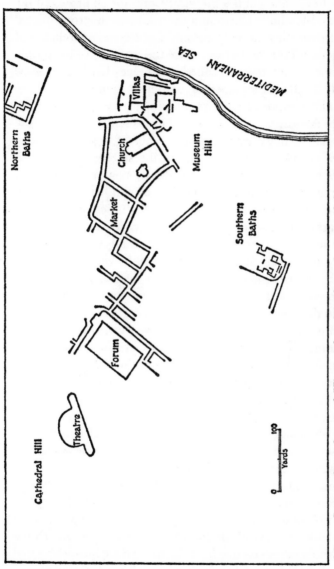

Map 3. Street plan of central Hippo, showing the only part of the town visible today. The coast is marked as it was in Augustine's time. Much land has been reclaimed since then. A main road now passes close to the villas, Museum Hill and the southern baths. A minor road goes over the theatre. Between the forum and the southern baths a large area was once excavated but has become overgrown again.

tion after the year 300, leading to the extraordinary triumph of the Church when the Emperor Constantine professed the faith and Catholic Christianity acquired such strong official support that it gradually became the recognised religion of the Roman Empire. In due course the majority of the people abandoned idolatry and called themselves Christians, some with full understanding, others with little or none.

Idolatry survived, but as a dying cause. At Madaura, where Augustine had once gone to school, people still thronged to pay homage at the tombs of legendary Punic heroes or offered sacrifices before the statues of numerous deities in the market place. An elderly pagan of Madaura, who regarded Augustine as a deluded man, wrote to him in defence of idolatry, arguing that 'through these gods all men with apparent discord but real harmony revere Him Who is the common Father of the gods and of all mortals'. Indignantly he demanded, 'Show me plainly who is that God whom you Christians claim belongs specially to you and whom you pretend to see present among you in secret places. It is in the open day, before the eyes and ears of all, that we worship our gods.' Such views, however, were destined to be submerged by an irresistible flood of Christian ideas.

This by no means meant that Augustine was faced with a simple religious situation, for it was not the profession of Christianity as such which was supported by the state but strictly Catholic Christianity. The Arian Church, differing from Catholics mainly in its understanding of exactly who Christ was, remained beyond the pale. The strife Augustine had witnessed in Milan showed that Arianism could stir deep passions and range armed men around a Catholic Church. But it was not strong in Africa, where the chief problem facing Catholics was the indigenous Donatist Church, a rather successful rival whose stronghold was Numidia. Donatists were not regarded as heretics, for in doctrine they agreed with the Catholic Church precisely. But in 311 they had separated themselves when they refused to accept Caecilian as bishop of Carthage, in the belief that one of those who consecrated him had surrendered copies of the Scriptures to the authorities during the persecutions. So they were schismatics and to the leaders of the Catholic Church in the fourth century this was a sin against God. There could be no question of mutual recognition or friendly cooperation.

Optatus, Catholic Bishop of Milevis near Cirta, writing fifty years after the event, described the Donatist Church as the product of anger, ambition and avarice, attributing the original dispute over Caecilian to Lucilla, a rich woman whom he had rebuked. In his history of the movement he stated that, thanks to Lucilla's bribes, a member of her household had been consecrated as rival bishop of Carthage. This man died shortly afterwards and was succeeded by Donatus, sometimes referred to as Donatus the Great, who led the breakaway church for the next forty years and according to Optapus 'seemed to himself no longer man but God'. These statements have too often been taken for the sober truth, because all Donatist accounts of their Church perished long ago. They should be treated with grave suspicion as the verdict of one of the movement's bitterest enemies, always imputing the worst motives to Donatists and the best to Catholics. No responsible Donatists would have accepted his version of events, for they were originally puritans reacting against the worldliness of the official Church. Their appeal to the common people was immense and before long they outnumbered Catholics in many areas, particularly in Numidia. Elderly people could tell Augustine that Donatists had once so predominated in Hippo itself that they refused to bake bread for the few Catholics who were left. To some extent it was also a movement in which Berbers expressed their desire to be Christians without being Romans. And persecution by the state Church only increased its resilience, confirming Donatists in the rightness of their cause and proving to them the utter corruption of Catholicism. No wonder Augustine wept when he was summoned out of his isolation at Tagaste to step into the centre of the Numidian stage.

Once persecution of the Church by the state ceased, the newly Christianised state began to persecute dissident Christians. Force was used against the Donatists as early as 317, but the worst events occurred in 347, not long before Augustine was born, when the Emperor of the day sent a heavy-handed envoy named Macarius to Africa to enforce Church unity. He had a lot of money to give away and Donatus was at once suspicious. 'What has the Emperor to do with the Church?' he asked and warned all his people not to be taken in. Macarius and his party travelled down into south Numidia, the heartland of Donatism, and approached the town of Bagai near the Aures Mountains. The local Donatist bishop turned his church into a fortress and prepared for the worst. Then, in the language of Optatus of Milevis, 'those who had brought the treasure to distribute among the poor conceived the plan, in such extreme necessity, of asking for soldiers'. Ten Donatist bishops, sent to confer with Macarius, were tied to pillars and flogged. The church was stormed and all its defenders massacred. Other leaders were killed or expelled and Donatus himself spent his last eight years in exile. Many towns which had been Donatist, including Tagaste, found it expedient to become Catholic. Yet the movement not only survived but went from strength to strength. All who had suffered in 347 were remembered as martyrs, while Catholics were commonly referred to as 'Macarians'. To this history and to these attitudes Augustine now fell heir.

A chance for independent action soon presented itself. Valerius was out of town one day when Augustine learnt that Maximin, the Donatist bishop of a place called Mutugenna, had rebaptised a Catholic deacon who had then become a deacon in the Donatist Church. Augustine strongly disapproved of a second baptism. Donatists who became

Catholics were not rebaptised, for Augustine regarded baptism as a rite instituted by Christ Himself which could not be invalidated by the imperfections of the person who administered it. Donatists, on the other hand, considered Catholics to be such wicked and polluted men, such deluded enemies of the gospel, that they did not recognise Catholic baptism at all. They claimed not to be rebaptising Catholics who joined them but to be giving them pure baptism for the first time. On this occasion, however, since he had received rather favourable reports of Maximin's moderation, Augustine wrote to him in a conciliatory tone :

'My beloved brother, I beseech you have the kindness to reply to this letter telling me what has been done, knowing that I intend to read your letter aloud to our brethren in the church. This I have written lest by afterwards doing what you did not expect me to do, I should give offence.' His hope was that his own letter and Maximin's reply might be made public as a step towards ending 'this schism, which is such a grievous scandal, causing Satan to triumph and many souls to perish'. However, he promised not to do this till after the departure of some soldiers who were in Numidia at the time. The events of 347 had never been forgotten and Donatists were always apprehensive lest Catholics call the state to their aid, just as Catholics dreaded the interference of bands of lawless men known as Circumcellions from their guerrilla-like way of life, moving around the farms, hamlets and chapels in the mountainous outback of Numidia. They had first appeared as a Donatist defence force in 347 and from that time the Roman authorities had to reckon with these elusive freedom fighters who did not necessarily share the Christian faith of the Donatist churches.

It was far from easy to distinguish religious dissent from political activism, but Augustine assured Maximin that he intended to rely on debate rather than violence. 'I do not propose to compel men to embrace the communion of either party,' he declared. 'On our side there shall be no appeal to men's fear of the civil power and on your side let there be no intimidation by a mob of Circumcellions.'

But nothing came of his efforts at reconciliation. A few kindly words were powerless to obliterate grim experience or wash away the blood of martyrs. And Maximin must have realised he would have no chance in debate with the ex-professor.

Chapter Nine

OLD MAN'S ASSISTANT

In childhood Monica had tried drinking wine secretly in
the cellar at Tagaste, but at Hippo Augustine found public
opinion had become so tolerant of drunkenness that it was
even permitted in church. Shortly before the annual feast
day in honour of a former bishop he preached an aggressive
sermon against this relaxation of morals, bluntly stating that
drunkenness was sin and drunkenness in church a crime.

Not very many were present, but the news of what he had
said spread through the town and aroused such hostility that
a large crowd assembled to listen to him on the day before
the feast. Helpers stood close by with Bible manuscripts open
at passages he had selected, ready to hand them to him. His
graphic account of what followed reveals the seriousness with
which he took the task of expounding the word of God and
the secret of the immense influence he soon came to wield. In
a tense atmosphere he talked for a long time about not turning the house of God into a den of thieves, skilfully analysed
the drunken revelry of the Israelites described in Exodus
chapter 32 — 'I took the manuscript from the attendant and
read that whole passage' — and in a commanding manner
enforced upon his hearers numerous Old and New Testament verses, including Paul's statement that drunkards will
not inherit the kingdom of God. He then reminded them of
Christ's humiliation, His pierced hands and crown of thorns,
His cross and His blood. 'In this appeal I put forth all the
power in thought and utterance which our Saviour and
Ruler was pleased to supply in so great and hazardous an
emergency. I did not move them to weep by first weeping
myself; but while these things were being spoken I own that,
moved by the tears which they began to shed, I myself could

not refrain from following their example. And when we had thus wept together, I concluded my sermon with full persuasion that they would be restrained by it from the abuses I had denounced.'

Next day, however, the outlook was less hopeful, for many resented the prohibition of celebrations to which they had become accustomed. 'Then the Lord showed me that He does not leave us alone.' The very men who were most vocal in opposition came to him privately before he had to speak in public and by talking to them in a kindly way he won them over to his viewpoint. Fortified by their support, he abandoned the message he had intended to give. Instead he explained to the people how these revels had originated after persecution ceased earlier in the century and large numbers of pagans entered the Church, who then celebrated Christian festivals in much the same way as they had heathen ones. He urged them to imitate overseas churches in this matter, but at that they appealed to the 'daily excess in the use of wine in the church of the blessed apostle Peter'. Augustine had to admit how difficult it had proved to suppress the evil at Rome because in such a city there were many carnally-minded people. 'If we want to honour the apostle Peter, I continued, we ought to hear his words and look more to the epistles by which his mind is made known to us than to the place of worship by which it is not made known', and he skilfully reinforced his argument by reading to them 1 Peter 4 : 1–3 with its repudiation of drunken revels. He then called everyone together at noon to celebrate the festival not by self-indulgence but by the reading of the word of God and the singing of psalms.

A very large company assembled. The reading and singing took place before Valerius and Augustine entered the church. 'Then the old man constrained me by his express command to say something to the people, from which I would rather have been excused as I was longing for the close of the anxieties of the day. I delivered a short discourse to express our gratitude to God.' As he was doing so the noise of revelry floated over to them from the nearby Donatist Church. 'I remarked that the beauty of the day is enhanced by contrast with the night.'

Before long the inevitable happened : Valerius asked him to preach on Sundays. Once launched upon this task he gathered up all the experience of his darker days and discovered a satisfying outlet for the findings of his Bible study. The result was an avalanche of sermons, taken down by secretaries as they were delivered, about a thousand of which are still available today.

Valerius was delighted. He was himself a Greek whose knowledge of Latin was so slight that it had proved to be of little use to him. He regarded the coming of Augustine as an act of God in answer to his prayers for the renewal of the Church through sound instruction. It was unknown in Africa for someone else to preach when the bishop was present and he was criticised for allowing it. But he knew it was customary in the East and he saw the people needed it, so he gave Augustine his full support and encouraged him to hold public discussions in church as well. This policy was dramatically vindicated in August 392. There had been a movement towards Manicheism ever since a man named Fortunatus, whom Augustine had known in Carthage when he himself was a Manichee, had begun preaching in Hippo. In a most unusual act of cooperation both Catholics and Donatists asked Augustine to confront him in public debate. From previous knowledge of Augustine, Fortunatus was rather anxious at the prospect, but his followers were so enthusiastic that he could hardly refuse. For two days they argued before a large audience in the Baths of Sossius. 'I affirmed that the evil of mankind had sprung from the choice of the will. He on the other hand tried to show that the nature of evil is co-eternal with God.'

In the end Fortunatus withdrew on the plea of consulting his colleagues, left the city at once, and never returned. Such a triumph spread Augustine's fame throughout North Africa and overseas. It was a difficult time for Catholic Christianity, challenged not only by Manicheism but also by the successes of the Donatist Church which was rebaptising large numbers of Christians. To have such a redoubtable champion as Augustine step into the arena was like life from the dead. His books and booklets were eagerly read and copies of his sermons widely distributed. 'So much authority was attributed to me that whenever it was necessary for someone to speak to the people and I was present, I was seldom allowed to be silent and listen to others.' He was also constantly teaching those who lived with him in the monastery which Valerius had encouraged him to establish alongside the church, where he was already training a number of dedicated men whose influence was destined to be far-reaching.

Valerius grew older and his health began to fail. He became so anxious lest some other town succeed in taking Augustine as its bishop that for a time he sent him away into hiding. Then a better plan occurred to him. He wrote to Aurelius, the new bishop of Carthage and primate of Roman Africa, suggesting that Augustine be made assistant bishop of Hippo. Aurelius, who already knew Augustine, gave his consent. Not long afterwards Megalius, bishop of Calama and primate of Numidia, came to Hippo with other prelates. Megalius had had doubts about Augustine, not being absolutely sure he had broken with his previous immoral way of life. However, Valerius persisted with his plans and eventually complete agreement was secured. Augustine himself, however, remained hesitant, believing it to be contrary to the custom of the Church to have two bishops in one town, but at length he was induced to consent. Only later did he learn that such an arrangement had indeed been prohibited by the Council of Nicea in 325, but at the time no one remembered this.

Alypius had become bishop of Tagaste a little earlier and it was he who sent five of Augustine's books to Paulinus, a wealthy official recently turned ascetic and preacher, who had been ordained by popular demand in Barcelona and moved with his wife Therasia to Nola near Naples. Describing himself as 'a veteran in the ranks of sinners but an untrained recruit in the service of the King eternal', he wrote enthusiastically to Augustine, sending a loaf of bread along with his letter as token of fellowship. 'You see, my beloved brother, esteemed in Christ our Lord,' he wrote, 'with what intimacy I claim to know you, with what amazement I admire and with what love I embrace you, seeing that I enjoy daily converse with you by the medium of your writings and am fed by the breath of your mouth. You have armed me completely by this your Pentateuch against the Manichees.'

An exchange of letters was extremely difficult when there was no postal service : it depended on finding a traveller willing to act as postman and the only hope of an early reply was for the same man to bring one back. Paulinus seized the chance to write a second time when two young men, 'most dear to us in the Lord', were going to Hippo. They gave Augustine a first-hand account of Paulinus so that 'by their very faces and eyes while they spoke I could with unspeakable joy read you written on their hearts'. He conceived the idea of getting Paulinus and Therasia over to Africa, for they had renounced normal married life and were living together as brother and sister, an example Augustine would have liked his congregation to see. He too sent a loaf of bread with his reply. And so, by the strong light shining out of Numidia, leading men everywhere became aware that a new star of the first magnitude had risen in the Christian sky. When the African bishops assembled for a general council at Hippo under the presidency of Aurelius in December 393, Augustine was given the opportunity of addressing them. His talk contained some seventy quotations from the Bible.

That same year he had been working on the book of Genesis. At Tagaste he had attempted an allegorical interpretation of it, but then he decided to add an explanation of its literal meaning. 'I wanted to test my capabilities in this most taxing and difficult work, but in explaining the Scriptures my inexperience collapsed under the weight of so heavy a load and before I had finished one volume I rested from this labour which I could not endure.' He switched his attention to the Sermon on the Mount and in 394 produced a commentary on it, devoting an average of half a page to every verse. Then, while in Carthage during the heat of summer, he delivered a series of addresses on the Epistle to the Romans and wrote a book answering the questions people put to him afterwards. Encouraged by this, he added a brief commentary on the Epistle to the Galatians, giving a simple explanation of each verse. Next he turned back to the Epistle to the Romans, planning to expound the whole of it in the same way, but once again found that he did not have the gifts such work demanded. 'Discouraged by the magnitude and labour of the task, I stopped.' Having covered only the first seven verses, he confessed with relief, 'I lapsed into easier things.' This was a pity, for such study would have been a helpful influence upon his subsequent life and teaching. Yet he was no doubt right in thinking that his talent was for the pastoral application of Scripture rather than for detailed, scholarly exposition, for which his ignorance of Hebrew and limited knowledge of Greek were severe handicaps. Yet it remains remarkable that he never again found time or inclination to comment systematically on any of Paul's Epistles. Instead he began to turn his powerful pen against the Donatists. The very first of his long series of polemical writings was a rhyme arranged according to the letters of the Latin alphabet. Its aim was to familiarise uneducated people with the issues dividing the established Catholic Church from the challenging 'Free Church'. It had a refrain, occurring no less than twenty-two times : 'All you who delight in peace now judge what is true.'

Chapter Ten

IN TOUCH WITH JEROME

It was during these first years at Hippo that Augustine began to correspond with Jerome, the greatest Christian scholar of the age. They had narrowly missed one another in Italy. Jerome had been in Rome when Augustine first visited the city and during the early part of his stay in Milan. But by the time of Augustine's conversion he had left the West to spend the last thirty-four years of his life at Bethlehem, from which he poured out an astonishing stream of Bible translations and commentaries. He was Augustine's senior by twenty-three years and thus an exact contemporary of Monica. As linguist and scholar Jerome also far surpassed the assistant bishop of Hippo. He had already embarked upon the titanic task of producing a new translation of the Old Testament from the original Hebrew which, along with a revision of the Gospels, was to form the basis for a new Latin Bible. The one in use in the fourth century is known to us now as the Old Latin, for it was eventually displaced by Jerome's masterpiece, which came to be called the Vulgate.

In 394 Alypius actually visited Bethlehem. 'When he saw you there,' wrote Augustine to Jerome, 'I was seeing you myself with his eyes, for anyone who knows us may say of him and me that we are two in body only, not in mind, so great is the union of heart, so intimate the friendship between us, though in merit we are not alike, for his is far above mine.'

Nevertheless, Augustine's first letter to Jerome was on several counts less than successful. Claiming to speak on behalf of all who were devoted to study in the African churches, he urged Jerome to give priority to putting Greek Bible commentaries into Latin and thus make them available to a wider public. He felt this would be much more useful than producing a new Latin Bible, unless Jerome clearly indicated the difference between any personal version of his own and the Greek Old Testament, the Septuagint, believed to be the product of seventy scholars and further hallowed by the numerous quotations from it in the New Testament. He made no secret of his greater confidence in the Septuagint, and in the Old Latin version translated from it, than in whatever Jerome might produce. 'I cannot sufficiently express my wonder that anything should at this date be found in the Hebrew manuscripts which escaped so many translators perfectly acquainted with the language.'

Moreover, Augustine took exception to Jerome's exposition of Galatians 2 : 11–14 in the commentary he had written on that Epistle. Augustine's view of these verses was that Peter was in the wrong in the incident at Antioch and Paul corrected him. Jerome had stated that Paul thought Peter was right but said and wrote that he was wrong 'in order to soothe troublesome opponents'. Augustine felt this was a disastrous suggestion, for it implied that it could be the duty of the author of a book in the Bible to deceive his readers, thus 'shaking our confidence in the authority of the Divine Scriptures'. He went so far as to accuse Jerome of lacking reverence for the sacred books and not having 'a profound persuasion of their truth'. He even allowed himself to describe this as criminal madness. The relationship between the two men was permanently bedevilled by this letter.

It proved no simple matter to find someone who could 'diligently keep, promptly bear and faithfully deliver' the letter to Bethlehem. A responsible friend of Augustine's named Profuturus was going that way. Copies were made and the original entrusted to Profuturus along with some of Augustine's other writings which he wanted Jerome to evaluate critically, confessing, 'I have the greatest difficulty in exercising a right judgment when I read over what I have written.' Unfortunately, just as Profuturus was about to embark, he was appointed bishop of Cirta, so his trip had to be cancelled. Shortly afterwards he died, and nobody knows what happened to the original letter. The copies of it were carried far and wide across Europe, bringing their strictures on Jerome to friend and foe alike, but not to Jerome himself.

Augustine was then in touch for the last time with Romanianus, whom he had good reason to describe as 'one of my dearest friends'. He was again visiting Italy and undertook to deliver a letter to Paulinus of Nola. In this Augustine warned Paulinus against taking Romanianus' praises of himself at their face value. 'I have often observed that without intending to say what was untrue, he was by the bias of friendship mistaken in his opinion concerning me.' Licentius, who had been present at Cassiciacum, was travelling with his father. Distressed by the boy's disorderly life, Augustine urged him not to surrender himself to Satan but to contact Paulinus, turn to Christ and accept His yoke. And with that, both men vanish from our sight.

During the five years when Augustine was assistant bishop of Hippo, the western half of the Roman Empire continued its long slide into chaos. Justina died not long after her son, Valentinian II, regained his throne from Maximus thanks to the help of Theodosius. Without her Arian influence, Valentinian became more favourable to Catholic Christianity. When he was twenty-one years old he asked Ambrose to baptise him, travelling to meet him at Vienne in France. At the same time he decided to dismiss the barbarian officer named Argobast who was then commander-in-chief in France. The upshot was that, while Ambrose was on his way to Vienne, Valentinian suddenly died, presumably murdered by Argobast. Instead of baptising him, Ambrose preached at his funeral in Milan.

For the moment Argobast was in power. He installed an Emperor named Eugenius and proceeded with the restoration of paganism, so when Eugenius entered Milan Ambrose thought it expedient to withdraw from the city. However, in 394 Theodosius intervened again, killed both usurpers and arrived in triumph in Milan. Prospects for responsible government looked good as the two halves of the Empire were reunited under this capable man. But tragedy was close at hand. Only four months later Theodosius died at the age of forty-nine, asking for Ambrose at the last. The fourth volume of Gibbon's *History of the Decline and Fall of the Roman Empire* opens dramatically with the words, 'The genius of Rome expired with Theodosius.' Imperial authority in the West again passed to a minor, his nine-year-old son Honorius.

And twelve months later, in faraway Numidia, bishop Valerius expired too and Augustine found himself sole bishop of Hippo in an Empire doomed to collapse before the hammer blows about to be rained upon it.

Chapter Eleven

CROWDS OF COMMON PEOPLE

The duties of the bishop of Hippo were different from what the title might imply today. 'My special charge does not extend beyond the Church of Hippo,' explained Augustine. 'In other towns I interfere with the affairs of the Church only so far as is permitted or enjoined by my brethren bearing the same priestly office, the bishops of these towns.' In spite of some oversight of the surrounding villages, frequent visits to Carthage and regular attendance at councils of bishops held in various towns, he was primarily the minister of one city church, occupied in the pastoral care of its large congregation and in a heavy programme of preaching, teaching and writing. In tracing the story of his life it should be remembered that in those days 'bishop' generally meant little more than the title 'Rev' nowadays.

However, Augustine was a prominent figure in the city as well as in the church. To begin with he had obtained the consent of the people to his request that he should be left undisturbed to study the Scriptures for five days every week. After a very short time the agreement became a dead letter. He was so regularly required to settle disputes about money, property or cattle that he often felt weakened in the discharge of his directly Christian responsibilities by 'the darkness and confusion arising from secular occupations'. He envied the monks who had isolated themselves on an island off the coast of Sardinia. 'I can scarcely breathe for the pressure of such duties imposed upon me.' His mornings were mostly spent sitting in court as an arbitrator, for in this way he could prevent Christians bringing legal actions before unbelievers. Sometimes he would devote an entire day to examining case after case, without even stopping for food. But, however irksome the task may have been, it provided admirable preparation for his preaching by giving him profound insight into the lives of those he addressed in church.

Year after year he had remarkable opportunities to influence people. Upon scores of them he conferred a touch of immortality by the verbal snapshots with which his books and sermons are littered : entertainers dancing on the tightrope, gamblers angry with their dice, physicians highly trained but rarely ill themselves, householders teaching their parrots to make jokes, barbers working with hair accumulating round their feet, spectators sitting in the sun in the amphitheatres to watch blood spilt, oarsmen singing their boatsongs in unison on the river, ornithologists imitating the chirping of different birds, women improving their complexion with make-up, highway robbers lying in ambush all night whatever the weather, wealthy landowners unable to sleep for fear of thieves, humble fellows hired to watch crops after dark, simpletons storing grain in a damp place, slaves grooming horses and cleaning out drains, parents abandoning their children to be picked up by some passer-by, wives not liking to be left alone or beaten by their husbands for looking out of the window too much, men flogged for kissing other men's wives, youths apparently possessing the characteristics of both sexes, old men who had never experienced even the mildest fever, women with breast cancer wondering whether surgery might prolong their lives, a writer breaking his reed pen in irritation at his own mistake, a villager carelessly walking in the dark towards an open well, a high-ranking lady persuaded by a Jew to improve her health by wearing next to her skin a ring threaded on a girdle of hair, a retired official who hoped to ward off evil influences by hanging up in his bedroom some sacred earth from Jerusalem, a youth washing a horse in a river at the height of summer, and a Christian lunatic who patiently put up with whatever the crowd said about him but pelted them with stones if they insulted Christ.

All these 'crowds of common people possessing no great strength of intellect', lay wide open to the Christian message. Idolatry was actively discouraged by the authorities, the Empire was visibly disintegrating, and the religion the state had adopted almost a century before offered a port in the world's storm. 'The name of Christ is on the lips of every man : it is invoked by the just man in doing justice, by the perjuror in the act of deceiving, by the king to confirm his rule, by the soldier to nerve himself for battle, by the husband to establish his authority, by the wife to confess her submission, by the father to enforce his command, by the rich man when he gives, by the poor when he receives, by the drunkard at his wine cup, by the beggar at the gate, by the good man in keeping his word, by the wicked man in violating his promises, all frequently use the name of Christ.'

In this situation Augustine was not alone. The Donatist Church was there too, and one day it chanced that his colleague Evodius met Proculeianus, the Donatist bishop of Hippo. As they talked together Evodius understood Proculeianus to say that he was willing to confer with Augustine in the presence of witnesses. The conversation was not entirely happy, for relations between the Churches were so chronically strained that Proculeianus thought Evodius had answered him insultingly. Augustine got in touch with him, apologising if the young man had spoken with undue excitement, and responded eagerly to the idea of a conference. He suggested they might hold it privately with an agreed report issued later, or with secretaries present. 'I willingly accede to whatever terms you wish.' He urged Proculeianus to join him in persevering prayer and peaceful discussion of every point at issue so that husbands and wives, parents and children, masters and servants might no longer be divided between the two Churches. 'What have we to do with the dissensions of a past generation?'

Distressing incidents repeatedly showed how desirable a better understanding between the Churches would be. One Catholic youth had taken to beating his widowed mother. He reacted angrily when Augustine tried to rebuke him, telling his mother he would join the Donatists and then drink her blood. He was duly rebaptised in a Donatist Church and Augustine became anxious lest he carry out the second part of his threat. Meanwhile a Catholic deacon from Spana had gone over to the Donatists along with two nuns with whom he was alleged to have had immoral relations. While travelling in the Spana district Augustine was loudly abused by a Donatist standing in a field and had to restrain his companions from laying hands on the man. He also intervened to prevent a farmer cultivating land belonging to the Church from beating his daughter into submission after she had been rebaptised and become a Donatist nun. Getting no response from Proculeianus about a conference, he appealed to a prominent Donatist layman. 'I cannot understand what there is in me, a novice,' he wrote, 'that should make him who calls himself a bishop of so many years standing unwilling and afraid to enter into discussion with me. If it be my acquaintance with liberal studies which perhaps he did not pursue at all, or at least not as much as I have done, what has that to do with the question in debate?' Augustine even suggested that another bishop named Samsucius should represent him for talks with Proculeianus — 'although unpolished in language, he is well instructed in the true faith'. However, the layman was not anxious to arbitrate between bishops and Proculeianus was not to be enticed into discussions in which he felt certain he would be worsted.

Problems which have troubled Christians in all ages were constantly brought to Augustine. 'As to killing others to defend one's own life, I do not approve of this unless one is a soldier or public functionary acting not for himself but in defence of others.' He maintained that the precept 'Do not resist an evil person' (Matthew 5 :39) was given to prevent us from taking revenge, 'not to make us neglect the duty of restraining men from sin.' And at a time when comprehensive insurance policies were not available he did his best to encourage those who were alarmed at the possibility of being held accountable if tragedies occurred. 'God forbid that we should be blamed for accidents which, without our desire, happen to others through things done by us or found in our possession which are in themselves good and lawful. In that event we ought to have no iron implements for the house or field, lest someone should by them lose his life or take another's; no rope or tree on our premises, lest someone hang himself; no window in our house, lest someone throw himself down from it; the oxen of a Christian should have no horns, his horses no hoofs and his dogs no teeth.'

In all his work in Numidia Augustine suffered from the handicap of speaking only Latin, a language imported five hundred years before when North Africa was annexed to the Roman Empire. Before 1000 B.C. the native tribes spoke various Berber or Libyan languages. When the coastal regions were penetrated by the Phoenicians they brought their own language, akin to Hebrew. Punic, the variety of Phoenician which became current in Africa, grew to be the mother tongue of many Berbers, but not of those in the mountainous interior which the colonists never dominated. Then came Latin, pushing Punic back as Punic had pushed back the native dialects. There was some overlapping, yet this threefold linguistic division of society—Berber, Punic and Latin—has to be borne in mind in evaluating the impact Augustine was able to make upon his contemporaries. The vastness of Numidia and the nature of its terrain ensured that there were limits to the influence of Roman culture, Roman language, and the Roman Catholic Church.

PART THREE

396–404
YEARS OF STRUGGLE AND FAME

Chapter Twelve

THE GREAT SCANDAL

Ambrose died in 397 and was succeeded as bishop of Milan by old Simplicianus, whom Augustine always remembered with gratitude. He himself was in poor health at the time. 'I am confined to bed. I can neither walk nor stand nor sit because of the pain and swelling of a boil. Pray for me that I may not waste my days through want of self-control and that I may bear my nights with patience.' The loss of Ambrose did not affect him much for they had never become close friends or corresponded since Augustine's return to Africa. But that same year a traveller brought him a letter from Jerome. It was only brief, for he had never had the letter Augustine wrote, and it reflected the political uncertainties which followed the death of Theodosius in saying that 'established here in our monastery we feel the shock waves on every side and are burdened with the cares of our lot as pilgrims'.

Augustine soon had an opportunity to reply, but reiterated his arguments against Jerome's exposition of Galatians, appealing to him to 'emend that book with a frank and truly Christian severity'. Most of Augustine's correspondents asked respectfully for his advice and he had just been writing to a young man concerned whether or not to fast on Saturdays. He told him that he expected all Christians to fast on Easter Saturday but that on other Saturdays only the church at Rome and a few other places fasted, sometimes adding Wednesday and Friday fasts as well. In some monasteries which fasted for five days every week, Saturday and Sunday were excluded. Fasting on Sundays he ruled out altogether as a Manichean custom. 'If I be asked what is my own opinion in this matter, I answer, after carefully pondering the question, that in the New Testament I see that fasting is enjoined, but I do not discover any rule definitely laid down by the Lord or the apostles as to days on which we ought, or ought not, to fast.' Accustomed to instruct others in this way, he carried over into his letter to Jerome the tone of a professor pointing out errors in the thesis of one of his students. To bishop Simplicianus he wrote with the utmost deference, inviting him to criticise his books, 'for I acknowledge the mistakes which I myself have made', whereas to Jerome, who was not a bishop and whom he knew only by repute, he adopted a slightly patronising attitude, assuring the older man that he approved of one of his books but then going on to criticise its title.

Because there was no postal service, writing letters was not a daily task for Augustine. What did confront him daily was the comparative weakness of the Catholic Church in Africa and the remarkable success of the Donatist Church, a success he was unable to view sympathetically since he regarded Donatists as criminals who had rent the Lord's tunic, which even his executioners had refrained from doing. He frequently quoted Psalm 2 :8, 'Ask of me and I will make the nations your inheritance and the end of the earth your possession', for he saw this fulfilled in the triumph of Christianity in the fourth century, during which the Catholic Church had increased and prevailed throughout the Roman Empire. He used the word 'Catholic' in its original sense of 'Universal', applying it proudly to the main Church which included such a large proportion of the population of the entire Mediterranean region, embracing all accessible parts of Europe, Africa and Asia. His delight at this was, however, matched by his distress that in Africa the Church had then been rent in two by 'the great scandal of schism'. To him the outstanding need of the time was the wiping out of this 'tumour'. All he could contemplate was the surrender of the other side, 'that they may have within the peace of the Church that holy sacrament for their salvation which they meanwhile have beyond the pale of the Church for their destruction'. Not for a moment could he consider mutual recognition and respect between Catholics and Donatists, even though he admitted they 'believe just what we believe'. Both Churches were episcopal, administering baptism and celebrating holy communion in the same manner. But the Donatist fellowship was less Roman than the Catholic Church and thus less European, less colonial, less confined to the Latin language. It had more simple, uneducated people, more country people, for its main strength lay back in the mountains, especially since the persecution of Macarius. The ecclesiastical division was affected by some social factors as well as religious questions, and these had their political repercussions for Gildo had long favoured the Donatists and one of his closest collaborators in his increasingly independent stance towards Rome was Optatus, the Donatist bishop of Timgad near the Aures Mountains. Under Gildo's favour and protection the Donatist Church continued to grow in numbers and morale. Then in 397 he virtually declared war on the Empire by preventing the departure of grain ships from Africa to Italy.

One exceptional Donatist, Tyconius, gained Augustine's respect thanks to his *Book of Rules*, which the bishop considered 'a very important aid towards understanding the Scriptures'. And it seems probable that it was Tyconius who sowed in Augustine's mind thoughts about the Church being the city of God on pilgrimage which were to bear fruit in the next century in one of his greatest books.

On one occasion Augustine discussed the question of disunity with a number of Donatist leaders at the town of Tubursi, going over with them the events which had led to the emergence of their Church some forty years before he was born. Not long afterwards he was there again and spent a whole day with the same men, reading to them from the civil and ecclesiastical records of the past with the aim of convincing them that the Church in which they had been brought up was no true Church at all. He had what he claimed were the facts at his fingertips and he was a scholar talking to countrymen from the mountains, ignorant of history. He told them all about Lucilla and her bribery and reminded them of the damage the Circumcellions, whose connection with their Church he did not doubt, were doing to the Roman population of Numidia. Having completed his indictment, he pointed the moral. 'Nothing compels you to remain in such fatal schism, if you would but subdue the lust of the flesh in order to win the spiritual kingdom and escape from eternal punishment. Go now and take counsel together. Find what you can say in reply.' Of course they could not find anything to say. They just waited till the great man had gone and then continued as before.

The following year Augustine was in Tubursi yet again. He got in touch with Fortunius, the Donatist bishop, suggesting a conference. 'He did not decline the visit. I therefore went to him, because I thought it due to his age that I should go to him instead of insisting upon his first coming to me.' Alypius and others were with him and they all sat down in Fortunius' house, which was then invaded by crowds of onlookers, few of whom came in a genuine spirit of enquiry. 'Everything was thrown into confusion by the noise of men speaking loudly.' After both Augustine and Fortunius had tried in vain to get them to listen in silence to the debate, a start had to be made under the most unfavourable conditions. 'For some hours we persevered, speeches being delivered by each side in turn so far as was permitted by an occasional respite from the voices of the noisy onlookers.'

Augustine tried to have the proceedings properly recorded but heckling was so bad that the secretaries gave up. In spite of this, the discussion continued. Each side accused the other of having surrendered copies of the Scriptures during the persecutions almost a century before. Augustine maintained that the Catholic Church was the true Church because it was to be found not only in Africa but throughout the Roman Empire. Fortunius maintained that his was the true

Church because of the persecutions it had endured at the hands of the Catholics when large number of Donatists were killed by Macarius' soldiers, churches confiscated and bishops exiled. He insisted that Augustine answer the question whether the persecutor or the one persecuted was in the right. He challenged him to produce a single New Testament example of a righteous man killing someone else. Many on both sides joined in the ensuing discusssion. 'We were by this time all standing, as the time of our going away was at hand.' Fortunius stated quite plainly that any Catholic going over to them must be baptised, but Augustine felt he said this with some regret and the conference ended with surprising cordiality. 'It was agreed by all that in such discussions the excesses of bad men ought not to be brought forward by either party against the other.' Warming to the old man, who had stood up to him so well, Augustine earnestly asked for his help in ending the schism. 'The next day he came to me himself and we began to discuss the matter again, but I could not remain with him as the ordination of a bishop required my departure.' Before he left Augustine suggested a longer conference with each side represented by ten men. To avoid the intrusion of onlookers, he proposed it be held in some village where neither party had a church. But nothing came of this idea.

Soon afterwards the Romans took action to destroy the power of Gildo. Having once used him to crush his brother Firmus, they now assembled an armada under his other brother Mascezel and when troops were landed Gildo's men melted away before the well trained legions. He himself escaped by sea but adverse winds drove him back to his death. The partisans were ruthlessly searched out and killed, bishop Optatus of Timgad among them. With these men perished the hopes of the North African nationalists and the respite they had provided for the Donatist Church came to an end. Ten years later imperial edicts were still striking fiercely at all who had sided with Gildo.

Chapter Thirteen

THE PREACHING BISHOP

As a man left the church in Hippo someone asked him what was going on inside. 'The bishop is speaking,' he answered. Week after week, year after year, many hundreds of people endured acute discomfort as they packed the church to hear Augustine. When he was a professor he had been a brilliant teacher and now he was a bishop he devoted himself unceasingly to the work of preaching. The teenagers who heard him in the fourth century were still listening to him when they were grandfathers. His sermons were biblical rambles: biblical, for they were exclusively concerned with the words of Scripture, with Christ and His Church, with Christian belief and behaviour; rambles, for they rarely fully explained any one text but passed quickly to many others drawn from all over the Bible, so that his talks were littered with hundreds of quotations. In this way his hearers acquired a knowledge of Scripture, for many could not read and very few possessed one of the bulky manuscripts of the Bible. He did not prepare the content of his messages in detail, nor keep to one subject, nor divide up his talks by clear headings, nor even tell Bible stories. His sermons were strictly spiritual, applying the word of God to the hearts of the people.

Like most of his contemporaries, including Jerome, he was more intent on drawing spiritual lessons out of Scripture than in establishing its original meaning, so that he often appeared to be a biblical magician who could produce gospel truth from the most unlikely passages. The five porches of the pool of Bethesda, for example, he likened to the five books of Moses, the water in the pool to the Jews, and the troubling of the water to the sufferings of Christ. In his hands

Map 4. Plan of Augustine's church in Hippo. Dots represent pillars and lines the remains of the walls. The rectangular part of the church is 53 yards long by 23 yards wide. To the left of it a trefoil chapel can be seen. To the right of it a smaller chapel opens, with the baptistry and its four pillars close by. It seems probable that Augustine lived within the area shown here.

the fig tree under which Christ saw Nathaniel denoted his sins, for it reminded Augustine of the fig leaves with which Adam and Eve covered themselves after they had fallen. As for the sycamore Zacchaeus climbed, 'Ascend the tree where Jesus hung for you,' he said, 'and *you* will see Jesus.' References to the moon in the Old Testament signified the Church, 'because she has no light of her own but is lighted by the Son of God, the Sun.' The shade of the gourd over Jonah's head prefigured the promises of the Old Testament, which was a shadow of good things to come; the worm which gnawed it represented Christ, who deprived those promises of their significance by fulfilling them, Christ the Worm who humbled Himself to become man, Christ the Morning Worm who rose from the dead before dawn. He could find mystic significance in Bible numbers, in 7, 8, or 10, in 40, 49, 50, 153, indeed in any number mentioned. In the Psalms the expression 'sons of Korah' meant Christians, for 'Korah is equivalent to the word "baldness" and we find in the Gospels that our Lord Jesus Christ was crucified "in the place of a skull".'

It would be easy to lengthen the list but quite wrong to imagine that because of such extravagances Augustine can be written off as a preacher of no significance, for a much larger collection of apt and powerful statements could be collected from his talks. He neatly divided Paul's hearers in the marketplace at Athens into mockers, believers, and doubters. 'Whoever mocks, falls : whoever believes, stands : whoever doubts, wavers.' Summarising the alternatives presented that day, he cried, 'Say, Epicurean, what makes you happy? "The pleasures of the body." Say, Stoic? "The virtue of the soul." Say, Christian? "The gift of God."'

As he began to elucidate the seventh chapter of the Epistle to the Romans, he appealed to his huge audience, 'Give me a patient hearing so that if, because of the obscurity of the subject, I have a difficult exposition, I may at least have an easy speaking. If both are difficult, my labour will be great.' He then proceeded to give them a talk packed with Scripture to an extraordinary degree. 'It is one thing not to lust and another not to go after one's lusts. Not to lust is the state of one altogether perfect : not to go after his lusts is the state of one fighting. In no other way can you be perfect in this life than by knowing that you cannot be perfect in this life. I speak of myself as perfect and not perfect at the same time.'

He was so well acquainted with the lives of his hearers, their sorrows and their sins, that he was able to lace his sermons with allusions which riveted their attention. He described how some men, weary of their business by the end of the day, would try to finish quickly and get home to rest, while others so dreaded returning to the friction in their families that they wandered about outside. He referred to farmers sweating on the threshing floors in the summer heat and to labourers staggering under heavy loads, panting and thirsting, hoping there were not robbers ahead. He depicted wealthy people not daring to keep money at home for fear their servants found it, preferring the bank, 'where everything is well taken care of', and greedy men enlarging their property by moving back boundary stones at night. And he revealed that while bread, wine, oil, wood and household goods were available in the market, some people found it so hard to pay their bills that they would even ask the bishop's advice how best to get hold of other people's property. He illustrated his messages by alluding to 'maidens of God', girls who had renounced marriage for religious reasons but then had to face a father's anger and a mother's tears; to slaves taking care not to give offence lest they be beaten, put in the stocks, or 'worn away at the mill'; to a man shivering in midwinter because his mistress told him she preferred him in lighter clothes; to a surgeon whose patient cried out in pain and struck him during an operation; and to a mother who softened little pieces of meat in her mouth before giving them to her infant son and then bore with his indignant cries as she 'rubbed him in the baths'.

The church was so crowded that tempers were often

frayed when fresh air was hard to come by and men trod on their neighbours' toes, but not everyone was really on Augustine's side. Many had already lost their hearts to the sporting heroes of the day, the charioteers. Others complained, 'I already live a good life. I commit no murder, no theft, no violence, no adultery, so why do I need Christ?' But they could all see his face and sense the appeal of his magnetic personality. 'Come, my brethren, catch my eagerness,' he would say, and their response was often electric—'your hearts I have not seen but I have heard your voices.' One day he was describing the toil involved in freighting merchandise to India. 'You don't know the Indians' language. They don't know you. Through perils you arrive; through perils you return. It was covetousness sent you to the Indies to bring back gold. How many, bearing these burdens, are calling out approvingly to me as I am speaking. If you call out, then lay aside what you are bearing!'

He never curried their favour. 'If you are about to marry,' he suggested, 'keep yourselves for your wives. As you would have them come to you, so ought they to find you.' And he knew the panic by which they could be gripped. 'You tremble; you grow pale, you run to the church, you want to see the bishop, you throw yourself at his feet. He asks, "Why?" You say, "Deliver me." "What is the matter?" "So-and-so is bringing a charge against me."' Having riveted their attention to such fears of other men's hostility, he abruptly asked what good reasons they should have for not committing adultery and at once answered the question himself. 'Because you fear hell, you fear the punishment of eternal fire, you fear Christ's judgment, you fear the society of the devil, lest you be punished with him and burn with him. Fear by all means. You can fear nothing better.'

He did not find it easy work. 'My preaching almost always displeases me. I eagerly long for something better, the sense of which I often enjoy in my mind, but then I am grieved when I find that I cannot express it adequately in words.' On one occasion he admitted, 'I have suffered much toil and anxiety. I sympathised with you and was anxious for myself, but to my thinking the Lord has assisted both you and me. If with all my pains I have been tedious to any of you, I have finished, and I congratulate you that the whole Psalm has been expounded. In the very middle of it, fearing lest I should burden you, I was about to let you go.'

Chapter Fourteen
THE MAZE OF DUTIES

As the fourth century drew towards its close, prospects for peace in the Roman world were not good. The most powerful man in the Empire was a soldier of fortune named Flavius Stilicho, a Vandal from eastern Europe. Proving successful in war and diplomacy, he was able to marry Serena, niece and adopted daughter of the Emperor Theodosius. After further victories over Picts and Scots in Britain, Stilicho and Serena became guardians of the child Emperor Honorius when, at the age of nine, he succeeded Theodosius in the West in 395. Three years later Stilicho got the boy to marry his twelve-year-old daughter Maria. Thus the fate of the Romans rested in his hands at a time when various tribes of Germany and central Europe were pressing with mounting force upon the long rampart of the Rhine which had for so many centuries kept them at bay.

By then Augustine had become a towering figure, whose knowledge and experience no one in Africa could match. Lesser men so hung upon his words that when he scribbled notes in the margin of his manuscript of Job someone got hold of it and distressed him by bringing them out as a book. Neither the clash of arms in Britain, nor slaughter on the Rhine, nor intrigues in Italy could disturb the tranquillity of lonely Hippo by the sea, backed by the Numidian mountains and the impenetrable Sahara.

As he worked at night in his study, or sat before the people massed in church, he could hear the waves breaking on the beach. Today the skeleton of Hippo, half-smothered in weeds and undergrowth, lies derelict on the edge of the Algerian town of Annaba (called Bône in the time of French rule), much of which was built on land reclaimed from the sea. In the fourth century the Mediterranean beat against the steep little hill now crowned by a museum. Hippo stretched along the shore where the road to Annaba airport runs, and inland to a higher hill on which an elaborate cathedral was erected by the French in the 1880s. Between Museum Hill and Cathedral Hill lie the bones of Hippo, partly buried under twenty feet of earth, partly excavated early in the twentieth century.

Looking out to sea, the view to the left was blocked by the towering mass of Mount Edough only a mile away, snow-capped in winter and a Donatist stronghold all the year round. Lower ridges enclosed Cathedral Hill on both sides. Only to the right across the mouth of the Seybouse River, the land lay open along the inhospitable, waterlogged coast stretching eastwards. In between the hills and ridges were small streams and marshy swamps, so that the town's natural defences were strong.

Close by Museum Hill was the church, able to take two thousand people standing, with the Donatist church just across the road. It is easy to see the actual spot in the centre of the apse where Augustine sat to preach on innumerable occasions. It takes only five minutes to walk round the block, treading on the huge stone slabs which were covering the central drain long before his day. In this block Augustine lived for much of his life, presiding over his group of dedicated celibates. Not far away lay the circular market and its adjacent shops, surrounded by extensive residential quarters with typically large Roman baths to north and south. Further inland stood the splendid forum with the theatre beyond it, utilising the steep slope of Cathedral Hill for its tiers of seats.

It was here in the last years of the century that Augustine wrote the most famous of all his books, the *Confessions*, in which he told the story of his life up to his mother's death. At once extremely popular, it has ranked high in the literature of the world ever since, enabling us to know him and Monica more intimately than most other figures in antiquity. At the same time he had already begun work on *The Trinity*, while a torrent of letters and shorter books flowed from his desk. Without parents to consider, with neither wife nor child to care for, he was able to devote his tremendous energy and exceptional talents to the needs of the people around him, to the city in which he was permanently anchored, and to the international Church he served. He took no holidays and had no leisure, yet he usually managed to preserve his health, speaking and writing with impressive freshness. His humility could also be impressive. 'So far am I from being acquainted with everything, that I read nothing in your letter with more sadness than this statement, both because it is manifestly untrue and because I am surprised you should not be aware that not only are many things unknown to me in countless other departments, but that even in the Scriptures themselves the things which I do not know are many more than the things which I know.'

Quite apart from the domestic and social problems brought before him daily in his capacity as an arbitrator, Augustine was never free from a maze of distressing situations plaguing the largely nominal Christian community of which he was the recognised head. A country congregation was in danger of being dragooned into accepting as their bishop a man who had already been officially deposed for misconduct. One of his colleagues began to read in church from books not in the accepted canon of Scripture. Some young men, tiring of his strictness, deserted his monastery and tried to get themselves ordained in Carthage on easier terms. One of the clergy was convicted of embezzling money with which he had been entrusted and was suspected of having 'dined and spent the night in the house of a woman of ill fame' on Christmas Day. A Donatist bishop, having acquired some property, rebaptised eighty Punic-speaking Catholic peasants whose landlord he had become. Augustine indignantly reminded him that a fine of ten pounds of gold could be imposed for such an outrage. 'How could you dare to transfer them in their ignorance to your communion?' he demanded.

When an elderly bishop named Victorinus invited him to go to a council of all the Numidian bishops, he found himself in an awkward position. The notice given was very short, the date clashed with other important engagements, and the summons reached him at a time when he was so ill that he could not think of accepting. In addition, his name was third on the list, 'although I know my proper place to be much lower down in the roll of bishops', while that of Xantippus was omitted altogether, 'whereas by very many he is regarded as the primate and it is he who issues such letters as you have sent.' So Augustine asked to be excused, suggesting the two old men send out a joint summons and put high on the agenda a decision about who, by virtue of seniority, had the right to be called the primate of Numidia.

In addition to coping with awkward people, Augustine grappled with problematical texts, including Christ's saying about the unforgivable sin, which he considered the most difficult in the whole Bible. For a long time he studied the problems it raised but deferred preaching on the subject, fearing that 'by words suggested at the moment' he might not do justice to his understanding of it. Then one Sunday he found himself listening to the twelfth chapter of Matthew in church. 'As the Gospel was being read,' he told the congregation, 'there was such a beating at my heart that I believed it was God's will you should hear something on the subject.'

In the sermon which followed he refuted the popular idea that when a Christian, one who had received the Holy Spirit and been baptised, was afterwards guilty of adultery or murder, he had committed the unforgivable sin. Augustine insisted that in these cases there was always the possibility of repentance, followed by forgiveness. He then expounded his own view that the only unforgivable sin was impenitence, because the unrepentant man 'stops the source of forgiveness against himself', but he qualified it by pointing out that so long as the person is alive, hope remains. 'How do you know whether he may not be a Christian tomorrow?' So he defined the sin against the Holy Spirit as impenitence till death. But then he added a further qualification. He claimed the Catholic Church alone possessed the Holy Spirit. 'All congregations, or rather dispersions, which call themselves Churches of Christ and are hostile to the congregation of unity which is His True Church, do not belong to His congregation just because they seem to have His Name.' In his opinion no sins could be forgiven outside the Catholic Church. From this he deduced that if someone who was not a Catholic repented of his sins but did not also repent of being 'an alien from the Church of God', his other repentance was of no profit to him and he was still guilty of the sin against the Holy Spirit. Thus the bishop of Hippo ended up by identifying the unforgivable sin with not being a Catholic.

Chapter Fifteen

THE VOICE OF FAUSTUS

Few of the first readers of Augustine's *Confessions* can have studied it with closer attention than Faustus, the Manichean bishop of Milevis, for it contained a vivid description of his own encounter with Augustine at Carthage in 383. Seventeen years later their paths crossed again. Faustus had written a book which Augustine considered to be against the true Christian faith. It has long since vanished but we still have Augustine's substantial reply in thirty-three chapters, each commencing with a quotation from the lost work introduced by the words 'Faustus said', followed by a lengthy section headed 'Augustine replied'. Thanks to this, the voice of Faustus can be heard to this day. Furthermore, his concern was not to proclaim his own views but rather to undermine Augustine's by attacking the credibility of the Bible on which his opponent's convictions were based.

Mani had claimed to be an apostle of Christ, so Faustus spoke as a Manichean Christian, though Augustine regarded him as a pseudo-Christian because, in addition to believing numerous Manichean superstitions, he did not accept the virgin birth of Christ, the doctrine of the incarnation, or even the fact that Christ really died. On his part Faustus treated Augustine as a semi-Christian whose faith was all mixed up with Judaism. He was a learned man with a remarkable gift for expressing himself effectively, a formidable critic of the Bible with a knowledge of the text of Scripture scarcely inferior to Augustine's, supporting all his arguments with apt quotations.

Faustus said : 'You ask me if I believe the gospel, though my obedience to its commands shows that I do. I have left my father, mother, wife and children, and all else that the gospel requires, and do you ask if I believe the gospel? Perhaps you do not know what the gospel is. The gospel is nothing else but the preaching and the precept of Christ. I have parted with all gold and silver and have left off carrying money in my purse, content with daily food, without anxiety for tomorrow. You see in me the blessings of the gospel. You see me poor, meek, a peacemaker, pure in heart, mourning, hungering, thirsting, bearing persecutions for righteousness' sake, and do you doubt my belief in the gospel? Let us ask Christ Himself. Who shall enter, O Christ, into Thy kingdom? His reply is, "he who does the will of my Father who is in heaven" (Matthew 7 :21) not "he who confesses I was born". Again, "You are my friends if you do what I command" (John 15 :14), not "if you believe that I was born". He nowhere says, "Blessed are those who confess that I was born." '

Faustus said : 'You ask if I believe in the Old Testament. Of course not, for I do not keep its precepts. Neither, I imagine, do you. I reject circumcision as disgusting and, if I mistake not, so do you. I reject the observance of Sabbaths as superfluous. I suppose you do the same. I reject sacrifice as idolatry, as doubtless you also do. I think all flesh unclean, you think none unclean : both alike, in these opinions, throw over the Old Testament. You cannot blame me for rejecting the Old Testament for, whether it is right or wrong to do so, you do it as much as I. The difference between us is that you choose to act deceitfully and to praise in words what you hate in your heart. I, not having learned the art of deception, frankly declare that I hate both these abominable precepts and their authors.'

Faustus said : 'Another reason for not receiving the Old Testament is that I am provided with the New, and Scripture says that old and new do not agree—"no one puts a piece of new cloth on an old garment, otherwise the rent is made worse." To avoid making a worse rent, as you have done, I do not mix Christian newness with Hebrew oldness. Another reason for not receiving the Old Testament is that if it was allowable for the apostles, who were born under it, to abandon it, much more may I, who was not born under it, be excused for not thrusting myself into it. The Old Testament promises riches and plenty and children and grandchildren and long life and the land of Canaan, but only to the circumsised, the Sabbath observers, those offering sacrifices and abstaining from swine's flesh. Now I, like every other Christian, pay no attention to these things, as being trifling and useless for the salvation of the soul. The Jews, satisfied with the Old Testament, reject the New, and we who have received the New Testament from Christ reject the Old. You receive both, and the one is not completed by the other but corrupted. Go on then as you have begun, join the new cloth to the old garment, put the new wine in old bottles, serve two masters without pleasing either, but allow us to serve only Christ. In the God of the Hebrews we have no interest whatever.'

Faustus maintained that the Old Testament was full of libels and shocking calumnies against God. It says 'he was greedy for blood and fat from all kinds of sacrifices, and jealous if they were offered to anyone but himself; he was enraged, sometimes against his enemies, sometimes against his friends; he destroyed thousands of men for a slight offence, or for nothing; he threatened to come with a sword and spare nobody.'

Faustus totally dissociated himself from the immoralities of David and Solomon, and from the behaviour of Abraham, 'defiling himself with a mistress with the knowledge of his wife, which only made it worse'; of Lot, 'who would have done better to perish in Sodom than burn with incestuous passion'; of Jacob and his wives, 'sometimes hiring him from one another for the night'; of Hosea, 'who got children from a prostitute and, what is worse, said that this disgraceful conduct was commanded by God'; and of Moses, 'who committed murder, waged wars, and commanded or perpetrated many cruelties'.

Referring to Christ's statement about sitting down with Abraham, Isaac and Jacob in the kingdom of heaven, Faustus said : 'We should be the last to grudge to any human being that God should have compassion on him and bring him out of perdition to salvation. Thus, in the case of the Jewish fathers who are mentioned by Christ in this verse — supposing it to be genuine —, although they led wicked lives as we may learn from their descendant Moses, or whoever was the author of the history called Genesis, which describes their conduct to have been most shocking and detestable, we are ready to allow that they may after all be in the kingdom of heaven, in the place which they neither believed in nor hoped for. But one thing perplexes me in your doctrine, why you are not of the opinion that the Gentile patriarchs also had a share in the grace of our Redeemer, specially as the Christian Church consists of their children more than of the seed of Abraham, Isaac and Jacob.'

Although Faustus accepted the New Testament in a general sense, he claimed the right to suspect the genuineness of any particular statement in it, 'to doubt whether Jesus ever said these words', and to question 'whether this is Christ's own declaration, requiring absolute belief from us, or only the writer's, to be carefully examined'. With regard to the saying of Christ that He came to fulfil the law, Faustus said : 'As a Manichean this verse has little difficulty for me, for at the outset I am taught to believe that many things which pass in Scripture under the name of the Saviour are spurious, and must be tested to find out whether they are true, for the enemy who comes by night has corrupted almost every passage by sowing tares among the wheat. So I am not alarmed by these words, notwithstanding the sacred name affixed to them, for I still claim the liberty to examine whether this comes from the hand of the good sower or of the evil one. But what escape from this difficulty can there be for you who receive everything without examination, condemning the use of reason, which is the prerogative of human nature, and as much afraid of separating between what is good and what is not as children are of ghosts?'

Faustus said : 'You have no right to claim from us an acknowledgement of the New Testament which you yourselves do not make for the Old. You cull out from the Old Testament only the prophecies telling of a future King of the Jews—for you suppose this to be Jesus—along with a few precepts of common morality, and all the rest you pass over. Why then should it seem strange that I select from the New Testament whatever is helpful for my salvation, while I set aside the interpolations of your predecessors which impair its dignity and grace. Besides, as we have proved again and again, the writings are not the production of Christ or His apostles, but a compilation of rumours and beliefs made long after their departure by some obscure semi-Jews and published by them under the name of the apostles, so as to give the appearance of apostolic authority to all these blunders and falsehoods. So it is not without reason that we bring a critical judgment to the study of Scripture. By examining everything and comparing one passage with another we determine what may or may not be genuine, taking with the help of the Paraclete the same liberties with the New Testament as Jesus enables you to take with the Old. There is no reason for you thinking it obligatory for me to believe all the contents of the Gospels, for you yourself take so dainty a sip from the Old Testament that you hardly, so to speak, wet your lips with it.'

Augustine resisted Faustus at every single point. He regarded the Old Testament as inspired by God just as much as the New, delighting to speak of their combination as a two-edged sword. Time and again he expressed his conviction that the New Testament lay concealed in the Old and that what the Old veiled the New revealed. 'The New Testament is latent in the Old : the Old is patent in the New.' At the same time he admitted that the New Testament was more important and valuable than 'the Jewish Scriptures', and that Christians were 'sons of the New Testament'. Faustus' opinions were to him 'a hateful mixture of ignorance and cunning' and he ominously expressed his surprise that 'the gentleness of Christian times allows such perverse iniquity to pass wholly or almost unpunished'. Item by item he did his level best to answer him, shirking nothing. He claimed to have gone over all the cases in which Faustus found fault with the Old Testament, to have fairly weighed each one, and then either to have defended the men of God or, where men were at fault, to have shown the excellence of the Scripture. He summarised his attitude in the statement that 'the precepts and symbols of the Old Testament contained both what was to be fulfilled in obedience through the grace bestowed in the New Testament and what was to be set aside as a proof of its having been fulfilled'.

Chapter Sixteen
THE DUEL WITH JEROME

About this time a man named Asterius set out from Bethlehem with an answer from Jerome to the letter Augustine
had written him five years previously. Only a copy of it had
eventually reached Jerome and he professed to 'refuse to
believe you to be the author of that which in another I would
sharply rebuke'. He observed that it was puerile self-
sufficiency for young men to try to gain glory for themselves
by attacking those who were famous. 'Do not, because you
are young,' he said, 'challenge a veteran in the field of Scripture. I have had my time and run my course to the utmost of
my strength. It is but fair that I should rest, while you in your
turn run.'

Unaware that Asterius was on his way, Augustine had a
chance to write again to Jerome by the hand of a friend
named Cyprian, but once more he adopted a critical tone,
urging Jerome to translate from the Septuagint into Latin
instead of working from the original Hebrew. He told him
that the bishop of Oea (now Tripoli in Libya) almost lost his
congregation after reading to them from Jerome's new translation of the book of Jonah, which used a different word for
'gourd' than the one with which they were familiar. Local
Jews had preferred the better-known word, so Augustine
rashly told Jerome he 'was led to think you may occasionally
be mistaken'. He made sure Cyprian took copies of all his previous letters to Jerome, and on one point at least he did submit himself to the old scholar. 'I wish you would have the
kindness to tell me what you think to be the reason for the
frequent discrepancies between the Old Testament text supported by the Hebrew codices and the Greek Septuagint ver-

sion, for the latter has no mean authority seeing it was the one which the apostles used in the New Testament.'

When Asterius reached Hippo with Jerome's letter, Augustine sat down to answer it in troubled mood. 'What hope is left of our engaging without bitterness in the discussion of scriptural doctrine?' Yet the blame was his and he knew it. 'It remains for me to confess as I now do, my fault as having been the first to offend by writing that letter, which I cannot deny to be mine. Why should I strive to swim against the current and not rather ask pardon? I therefore entreat you by the mercy of Christ to forgive me wherein I have injured you and not to render evil for evil by injuring me in return.' Realising at last what kind of man Jerome really was, he longed to sit beside him and learn from him. 'I have not now, and I can never hope to have, such knowledge of the Divine Scriptures as I see you possess,' he confessed. 'Whatever abilities I may have for such study, I devote entirely to the instruction of the people whom God has entrusted to me and I am wholly precluded by my ecclesiastical occupations from having leisure for any further prosecution of my studies than is necessary for my duties in public teaching.' Yet he was concerned at the vehemence of Jerome's letter, knowing the bitter animosity which had destroyed Jerome's friendship with his former colleague Rufinus, so he took the precaution of sending his answer via a trusted friend who was to add a covering letter and also frankly tell Augustine if he thought he had expressed himself unsuitably.

Their letters continue to cross, for soon afterwards Augustine had Jerome's answer to his less tactful letter in which he had suggested Jerome might sometimes be mistaken. The great translator, by then aged seventy-three, whose monumental new Latin Bible was about to be given to the world, was not a little perplexed to know how to cope with his critical correspondent in Africa.

'You are sending me letter upon letter,' he complained, 'challenging an old man, disturbing the peace of one who asks only to be allowed to be silent, and you seem to desire to display your learning.' He aptly described Augustine's original letter as 'a honeyed sword'. A friend of his had come across a copy of it on an island in the Adriatic.

'The same letter is reported to be in the possession of most of the Christians in Rome and throughout Italy, and has come to everyone but myself, to whom alone it was ostensibly sent.' He felt Augustine had set at nought the laws of brotherly fellowship and regretted that the world should see them quarrelling like children. 'It does not become me, who have spent my life from youth until now sharing the arduous labours of pious brethren in an obscure monastery, to presume to write anything against a bishop of my own communion, especially against one whom I had begun to love before I knew him, who also sought my friendship before I sought his, and whom I rejoiced to see rising as a successor to myself in the careful study of the Scriptures. Farewell, my very dear friend, my son in years, my father in ecclesiastical dignity. And to this I most particularly request your attention, that henceforth you make sure that I be the first to receive whatever you may write to me.'

Before Augustine's letter asking for forgiveness could reach Jerome, Cyprian was back from Bethlehem bearing a tremendous letter of self-defence and counterattack from the old man. It had been dictated in haste, as he complained Cyprian only gave him three days notice of his departure for Africa. 'Our armour is Christ,' he declared, marshalling many a scriptural quotation before getting down to business. 'I say nothing of the compliments by which you attempt to take the edge off your censure.' Then, with great vigour and remarkable command both of the biblical text and of earlier commentaries on it, he defended his view of the second chapter of the Epistle to the Galatians and in return charged Augustine with error in his understanding of Paul's attitude to the Mosaic Law. He appealed to him to 'refrain from stirring up against me the unlearned crowd, who esteem you as their bishop and regard with the respect due to the priestly office the orations which you deliver in the church, but who esteem lightly a decrepit old man like me'. He proceeded with unerring aim to demolish Augustine's objections to his Old Testament translations. 'You must pardon my saying that you seem to me not to understand the matter.' In spite of his ignorance of the Hebrew language, Augustine had for many years been expounding the Psalms in a series of sermons. Numbers of these came into the hands of Jerome, who had no difficulty in scoring off him linguistically over them nor in setting his mind at rest about Jonah's gourd.

When another man from Hippo turned up in Bethlehem a year later, Jerome was disappointed to find he had never told Augustine he was coming, so brought no letter, but he seized the chance to send a note back by him to soften the impact of his own retort. 'That letter was not an answer from me to you, but a confrontation of my arguments with yours. If it was a fault in me to send a reply—I beseech you, hear me patiently—the fault of him who insisted upon it was greater. But let us be done with such quarrelling. Let there be sincere brotherly love between us. Let us henceforth exchange letters not of controversy but of mutual charity. Let us exercise ourselves in the field of Scripture without wounding each other.'

This was a fine gesture, though Jerome made no reference to the letter in which Augustine had asked for his forgiveness, and unfortunately Augustine took offence at the word Jerome had used for 'exercise ourselves', literally 'let us amuse ourselves.' So he returned to the attack with a vigorous restatement of his view of the verse in Galatians, which in fact has been generally accepted ever since in preference to Jerome's. And he stoutly defended his opinion that 'in that time in which the grace of faith was at first revealed' it was permissible for Paul and others to continue observing some of the ceremonies of the Mosaic Law. 'These observances were to be given up by all Christians, step by step, but not all at once. It never was my opinion that in our time Jews who become Christians are at liberty to observe the ceremonies of the ancient dispensation.'

Though in the main he gave no ground, he did admit that 'in many things Augustine is inferior to Jerome' and he at last agreed that it was beneficial for Jerome to translate direct from the original Hebrew. He concluded by saying, 'I confess that I would not like any letter of yours to meet with the fate of which you justly complain as having befallen my letter to you.'

It was several years before either of them wrote again.

PART FOUR

404–411
YEARS OF CONTROVERSY AND MATURITY

Chapter Seventeen

THE LOVE OF MONEY

Augustine took little interest in financial matters and was content to delegate administrative duties concerned with property owned by the Church at Hippo. All he asked was to be shown an annual statement of accounts. But occasionally he could not avoid becoming personally involved.

He and Alypius had an anxious time deciding what to do after the death of a man named Honoratus who had been a member of their monastic group at Tagaste. He had expressed the wish to give to the monastery his property at Thiave, though the gift was never properly legalised. Later Honoratus became the minister of the Church at Thiave, which had formerly been part of the Donatist Church but then came over to the Catholics. The people of Thiave presumed the property still belonged to Honoratus, so when he died they expected to get it, in accordance with the custom that 'whatever belonged to an ordained clergyman in any place, belongs after his death to the Church over which he was ordained'. It was, however, possible to argue that the property had been gifted to the monastery, which had of course moved to Hippo. The two friends were slow to settle the matter and had too little time at their disposal when they did meet to discuss it. Alypius suggested, as a compromise, that half the property should go to the Church at Thiave and that the value of the other half should be made up to them in cash by Augustine. Together they agreed to resist the demand from Thiave that the whole property be handed over. However, this caused such distress, and made Alypius so unpopular, that Augustine could not get the matter off his mind.

'Fearing lest, as frequently happens, I should myself be mistaken through partiality for my own opinions,' he told Alypius, 'I stated the facts of the case to our brother and colleague Samsucius, mentioning the view taken by both of us. He was exceedingly shocked and marvelled that we had entertained such a view, moved by the ugly appearance of the transaction as one wholly unworthy not only of us, but of any man.' Thanks to this timely advice Augustine felt the only thing to do was to let the Church have the entire property, whatever the real rights and wrongs of the matter might be. He sent Alypius a letter for them, embodying this solution in both their names, urging him to send it on at once to Thiave unless he strongly disapproved.

It often happened that people made wills bequeathing money to the church for the relief of the poor. On occasion it fell to Augustine to refuse such legacies if he considered an injustice was being done to children, parents, or other relatives.

There was one man from Hippo, living in Carthage, who made some property over to Augustine personally, retaining the interest derived from it during his lifetime. Then he changed his mind, demanding the return of the legal documents and sending instead a small donation for the poor. Augustine decided to return to him both documents and donation. After that experience he felt it wiser to accept gifts from the dead rather than the living. He consistently refused gifts of money made to himself. If he was given gifts in kind, such as clothes, he accepted them only on the understanding that they were for the use of others as well. 'I will accept nothing for myself which is not to be of service to our community.' He was insistent upon this, for the clothes given to him tended to be expensive ones. 'Would you have men say that in the Church I found means to obtain richer clothing than I could have had in my father's house or in the pursuit of secular employment? If gifts of costly clothes are given to me, I shall sell them in order that the money realised by the sale may be a common benefit.' We know of only one exception that he made to this rule. A deacon of the church in Carthage, whose sister had made him a tunic, died. She sent the tunic to Augustine, saying what a comfort it would be to her to know that he was wearing it, and he felt it would be wrong to refuse her.

Not all bishops were successful in resisting the temptation to enrich themselves. Augustine was compelled to take disciplinary action in the case of Paulus, whose extravagant life style had become a scandal. 'I rejoice in the number who have, by God's blessing on your work, been gathered into the Catholic Church,' he wrote to him, 'but this does not make me less bound to weep that a greater number are being scattered from the Church by you. The office of a bishop is not designed to enable one to spend a life of vanity.' Paulus complained that Augustine just did not like him and was being influenced by men who had been against him all along. Augustine disagreed. 'It is by no means as you suppose.'

There was trouble in his own monastery too. A man who was already ordained reported another member of the community to Augustine for making 'an immoral and vile proposal' to him. The bishop was inclined to believe him, though he recognised that it might have been the ordained man himself who was at fault. The matter became so widely known that he had to issue a formal statement to the clergy, elders and people of the church in Hippo. In this he admitted that 'as I have hardly found any men better than those who have done well in monasteries, so I have not found any men worse than monks who have fallen'.

And the Donatist problem refused to go away. The danger grew that when bands of Circumcellions, motivated primarily by social and economic stresses, used violence against more prosperous and settled communities which tended to be Catholic, the official Church invoked the power of the state to crush the whole Donatist movement. Augustine still hoped for an amicable solution, based on 'the love of peace and the

logic of truth', though these expressions were only his euphe-
misms for surrender to the Catholic cause. He still clung to
his original view that it was not right to coerce schismatics
into the Catholic Church by force. Hearing good reports of
the character and learning of one of the Donatist leaders he
made approaches to him. With a delicate mixture of moderation and firmness he reiterated his conviction that Donatism
had committed a grave crime by separating itself from the
rest of Christendom. 'We do not lay any charge against you
but the one of schism.' Then he threatened him by quoting
Romans 13 : 4, 'If you do wrong, be afraid, for he does not
bear the sword for nothing,' claiming that this justified the
civil power in persecuting schismatics. He maintained that
people had to be protected against 'lawless acts of violence
perpetrated by individuals of your party, which you yourselves, who refrain from such things, bewail and deplore.'

Unfortunately the security situation continued to deterio-
rate so alarmingly that Augustine appealed directly to Januarius, the Donatist primate of Numidia. 'Your clergy and
your Circumcellions,' he alleged, 'are venting their rage
against us in a persecution of unparalleled atrocity.' He gave
details of bishops ambushed, clergy assaulted, laity blinded
by a mixture of lime and acid thrown in their eyes, houses set
on fire, granaries plundered, and a friend of his beaten up,
rolled into a muddy pond, and kept prisoner for two weeks.
Seeing his community threatened with clubs, swords, fire and
acid, Augustine felt increasingly justified in calling for state
protection against 'your worthless and diabolical schism'. Yet
he still proposed to Januarius that the bishops of both sides
should meet in conference. Failing that, he asked the primate
to send some responsible people into the district of Hippo
for an official investigation. And he warned him that if the
situation continued as it was, Januarius would regret 'that
you despised our humble attempt at reconciliation'.

Augustine himself was in danger from these attacks.
Among his opponents were some who argued that 'the wolf

should be slain in defence of the flock', suggesting that God would pardon any sin incurred by those who achieved this. One attempt to kidnap him was only prevented because his guide took a wrong road. On another occasion, homeward bound from Calama, his party was ambushed. Some of them were wounded and they lost a few animals.

Chapter Eighteen
THE VOICE OF PETILIAN

'Petilian, a bishop, to his well-beloved brethren, fellow-priests and deacons, appointed ministers with us throughout our diocese in the gospel, grace be to you and peace, from God our Father and from the Lord Jesus Christ.' So began an open letter from the Donatist bishop of Cirta to his colleagues, in which he spoke out strongly against the Catholic Church and Augustine in particular. Someone copied it for Augustine and he was urged at all costs to answer every point Petilian made. He explained that in his reply, 'I will set down the words of his letter under his name and I will give the answer under my own name, as though it had all been taken down by reporters while we were debating.'

Petilian was a very different adversary to Faustus. He lacked both the learning and the eloquence of the Manichean. But he articulated the simple, biblical faith of the Berber Donatists and gave vent to the indignation of the mountain Christians at the bitter hostility shown to them by the Catholic Church, of which Augustine was the outstanding spokesman. Intellectually he was really no match for Augustine at all. He did not so much set out reasoned arguments as shout his defiance and then fall back upon lengthy quotations from the Bible. At the outset he made clear his opinion of the distinguished bishop of Hippo. 'You wicked persecutor, under whatever cloak of righteousness you conceal yourself, under whatever name of peace you wage war with kisses, you are the true son of the devil, showing your parentage by your character. You falsely call yourself a bishop. To you the Lord Christ will say, "Depart from me, you cursed, into everlasting fire." '

Too often in succeeding centuries the Donatist Church has been despised and condemned on the testimony of Augustine. It is only right that we should listen for a while to what a Donatist leader thought of him. Petilian considered Augustine to be a murderer. 'Reckon up all the deaths of the saints —so often have you murdered Christ who lives in each of them. You, who call yourself a Christian, you do err, you do err, for God does not have butchers for His priests.' He quoted the whole of Psalm 1 against Augustine, then the whole of Psalm 23, then each of the Beatitudes from the Sermon on the Mount. 'On account of your wickedness the Lord does not know you. Your bloodstained conscience makes your prayers of no effect.' He harped on that word butcher— 'you, our butchers'.

Augustine defended himself with equal determination, denying everything Petilian had said, pouring scorn on him and his Church, blaming them for the extravagances of the Circumcellions, claiming that the Donatists were themselves guilty of the very crimes they attributed to Catholics and pointing repeatedly to the harshness with which they had treated splinter groups of their own. So there was no meeting of minds, no mutual sympathy, only stark confrontation as he replied at some length to the brief statements he selected from his adversary's letter.

Petilian insisted that the Donatist Church did not feel free to retaliate. 'You carry on war without licence, but we may not fight in return. Our victory is either to escape or to be slain. To us the Lord has commanded simple patience and harmlessness.' Indignantly he demanded, 'What is the justification for persecution? Jesus Christ never persecuted anyone. On what principle do you persecute?' When Augustine referred to Christian love and equated it with ecclesiastical unity, he struck back at once. 'Love does not persecute. Love does not inflame emperors to take away the lives of other men, does not plunder other men's goods, does not go on to murder those whom it has spoiled. Where is your Christianity if you order such things to be done? You do not cease to murder us, who are just and poor—poor, that is in worldly wealth, for in the grace of God not one of us is poor. For even if you do not murder a man with your hands, you do not cease to do so with your butcherous tongues. All who have been murdered, you, the instigator of the deed, have slain. Nor does the hand of the butcher glow save at the instigation of your tongue. What Cain the murderer did once, you have often done, in slaying your brethren.'

For more than ten years Petilian was to maintain his defiance. Augustine echoed the Catholic story about him, that he had been brought up in their Church but seized by the Donatists, who 'dealt violently with his unwillingness, tracked him down while in flight, discovered him in hiding, pulled him out in terror, baptised him quivering with fear and ordained him against his will'. On his part Petilian suggested that Augustine was still at heart a Manichean and blamed him for the introduction of monasticism to Africa, for not allowing other men to be Christians in their own way, and for promoting 'unity by war'. He assured Augustine that 'inasmuch as we live in the fear of God, we have no fear of the punishments and executions you wreak with the sword' and he optimistically proposed that the bishop should submit to be baptised by those whom he was persecuting. 'If you say that we give baptism twice over,' he declared, 'truly it is you who do this, slaying men who have been baptised, because you cause each one of them to be baptised in his own blood. For the baptism of water or of the Spirit is as it were doubled when the blood of the martyr is wrung from him. And so our Saviour Himself, after being baptised in the first instance by John, declared that He must be baptised again, not this time with water nor with the Spirit but with the baptism of blood, the cross of suffering. Blush, blush, you persecutors. You make martyrs like Christ, sprinkled with the baptism of blood after the water of genuine baptism.'

To this Augustine replied, 'We do not kill you, but you kill yourselves when you cut yourselves off from the living root of unity. If you have made a schism you are impious. If you are impious, you die as one guilty of sacrilege. If you die as one guilty of sacrilege, how are you baptised in your blood?' And he repelled the accusation of murder by an argument which enabled him to identify Donatism with spiritual murder. He stated that whoever separates from the only true Church is 'unable to defend himself from the charge of murder which is involved in the mere offence of dissension and schism, as the Scripture says, "Anyone who hates his brother is a murderer." (I John 3 : 15).' He justified the actions of the Catholic Church by reminding his opponent that Paul once delivered a man over to Satan for the destruction of his flesh so that his spirit might ultimately be saved. Referring to the expulsion of merchants from the temple with a whip, he deduced that 'we do find Christ a persecutor'.

So he tried to silence the voice of Petilian. And in subsequent ages that voice, like the voice of Faustus, has indeed been drowned by the orchestra of praise evoked by the genius of Augustine and by the odium poured upon all who disagreed with him. But in silencing the bishop of Cirta, the bishop of Hippo preserved his words and wrote his epitaph.

Chapter Nineteen

THE HARDENING OF THE MIND

A large, circular, Roman pool not far from the Algerian town of Guelma is a reminder of the importance in Augustine's time of the city of Calama, lying on the upper reaches of the Seybouse River surrounded by mountains. Possidius had become the local bishop. He was one of ten young men trained by Augustine in the monastery at Hippo and then ordained for service in other towns. Each of them continued the same pattern of work, establishing in his new sphere a fresh monastery which served as a small theological college where, 'encouraging arduous study based upon the Word of God, they prepared members of their brotherhood for the priesthood', not only in other parts of Roman Africa but even overseas.

In June 408, however, Possidius narrowly escaped an untimely end. In spite of legislation forbidding pagan festivals, a feast day had been observed in Calama, during which crowds of people passed along the streets and danced provocatively in front of the Catholic church. When the clergy tried to put a stop to this, the church was stoned. Possidius appealed to the authorities, but a week later the church was stoned again. Next day an unsuccessful attempt was made to bring the matter to court, after which, as soon as a hailstorm had subsided, a more serious attack was launched to set the buildings on fire. Those who were inside managed to hide or escape, apart from one man whom the rioters killed. Possidius 'lay folded double, listening to the voices of the ruffians seeking him'. The leading men of Calama did not intervene, though some unidentified stranger managed to rescue a number of those whose lives were in danger and to recover property looted in the excitement. Possidius was so alarmed at what had happened that before long he left to report the matter in Rome.

On reflection, the pagan community of Calama realised that retribution would probably be painful, so an elderly citizen named Nectarius was asked to approach Augustine on behalf of his people. 'There are many things in the colony of Calama which justly bind my love to it,' he wrote. 'I was born here and in the opinion of others I have rendered great services to this community. But now this town has fallen disastrously by a grievous misdemeanour on the part of her citizens, which must be punished with very great severity if we are dealt with according to the rigour of the civil law. But a bishop is guided by another law. His duty is to promote the welfare of men, to interest himself in any case only to benefit the parties and to obtain for other men the pardon of their sins at the hand of the Almighty God. So I beseech you with all possible urgency to make sure that the guiltless are protected and a distinction drawn between the innocent and those who did the wrong.'

Augustine's reply was rather cool, for he was anxious to deter anti-Christian rioters in future. While agreeing that there might be degrees of guilt and that those who were too frightened to take any action could be excused, he felt the success of a stranger in bringing help showed how guilty the local community had been. Eight months later Nectarius renewed his appeal. 'I implore you to consider again and again who you are, what is your professed character and what is the business to which your life is devoted. Reflect on the appearance of a town from which men doomed to torture are dragged away; think of the lamentations of mothers and wives, of sons and fathers; think of the shame felt by those who may return having undergone the torture; think what sorrow and groaning the sight of their wounds and scars must renew. And when you have pondered all these things, think of God, think of your good name among men, and seek to be praised not by punishing but by pardoning the offenders. May the supreme God be your keeper and preserve you as a bulwark of His religion and an ornament to our country.' Augustine replied to him at some length but maintained a certain aloofness in his reluctance to be told his Christian duty by a worshipper of Jupiter.

Far to the west, in the land then called Mauretania, lived Vincentius, an old friend of Augustine's pre-Christian days in Carthage. He had become the leader of the Rogatists, a tiny group which had broken away from the Donatist Church. Remembering Augustine as 'a man devoted to peace and righteousness when you were still far removed from the Christian faith', he was shocked to hear that the bishop now favoured the use of the secular arm in quelling Donatism and forcing people back into the Catholic Church. In Vincentius' view no one should be coerced in matters of faith. He challenged Augustine to produce a single New Testament example of 'any petition presented on behalf of the Church to the kings of the earth against her enemies'. Far from yielding to his arguments, Augustine set out in full his contrary convictions in a forty-five-page answer. 'It would have been much shorter if I had been thinking of you alone.'

He argued that Paul was compelled to embrace the truth 'by the great violence with which Christ coerced him' in making him blind on the Damascus road. 'Jezebel slew prophets,' he admitted but added, 'Elijah slew false prophets.' With the third chapter of the book of Daniel open before him, he maintained that the earlier period in the life of Nebuchadnezzar, when he demanded that the golden image be worshipped, 'represented the former age of emperors who did not believe in Christ, at whose hands the Christians had suffered because of the wicked', whereas the later period of Nebuchadnezzar's rule, when he made slander against God a capital offence, 'represented the age of the successors to the imperial throne, now believing in Christ, at whose hands the wicked suffer because of the Christians'.

Claiming that it is right to take a sharp knife away from a child and to tie up a madman, he laid down the principle that 'it is better with severity to love than with gentleness to deceive'. So he unashamedly explained to Vincentius the change that had taken place in his own thinking. 'Originally my opinion was that no one should be coerced into the unity of Christ, that we must act only by words and fight only by arguments, prevailing by force of reason. But this opinion of mine was overcome, not by the words of those who controverted it, but by the conclusive instances to which they could point. In the first place my own town, though it was once wholly on the side of Donatus, was brought over to the Catholic unity by fear of the imperial edicts.'

He claimed that there were large numbers of Circumcellions who had become Catholics and regarded their former convictions as a delusion. There were plenty of others who told him how glad they were that strong measures had cured them of their Donatist blindness. So he persuaded himself that to shock and alarm people by 'the force of fear', to repress them by 'terrors of a temporal kind', to punish them by fines, confiscation and exile, and to deny them freedom in their business transactions and wills, was all a valid expression of Christian love since it rescued them from the crime of schism. Henceforth he regarded it as right to employ 'the formidable power of the authorities of this world' to assist the Church by bringing back into the fold those whom family tradition, apathy, slander, or the notion that 'it did not matter in what communion we hold the faith of Christ' kept among the Donatists.

In Christ's parable of the Great Supper in Luke 14 he found a New Testament parallel to his understanding of the history of Nebuchadnezzar. At the beginning of the parable the servant is instructed to invite the guests, saying, 'Come, for everything is now ready.' This Augustine equated with the witness of the Church during the era of the pagan emperors prior to Constantine. Later in the parable the servant is sent out again and told to 'compel people to come in'. This he connected with the more favourable situation since the rulers of the Empire had professed the faith. Thus Augustine claimed the authority of Christ Himself for compelling others to enter the Catholic Church.

But he could not shake off a certain uneasiness, so when Possidius went to Italy after the riot at Calama, Augustine took the opportunity of sending a frank appeal for advice to Paulinus, whose understanding he sensed, though they had never met. The memory of Cassiciacum, the mirage of the perfect tranquillity of Christian retirement, still beckoned him. He longed to escape from the harsh arena of public affairs in the busy world. One of the texts he most frequently quoted was the first verse of the seventh chapter of Job, which in his version read, 'Is not the life of man upon earth a life of temptation?' He thought that, on his annual visit to Rome, Paulinus might fall in with 'some judicious spiritual physician' who could advise him further on how Christians ought to live amongst men. 'If anything has become known to you through experience or meditation, or if you have already found or can learn anything from other teachers, I beseech you to give me instruction. I am most eagerly longing to be instructed by you.' And beyond all that he wished for heaven 'where the evils which we experience here shall have no place'.

Chapter Twenty

UNDER THE SHADOW OF DISASTER

From the opening of the fifth century danger signals had been flashing in the Roman sky. Late in 405 Radagaisus, a pagan Goth from south-east Europe, led his men across the Alps and held the north of Italy for some months until overwhelmed by Stilicho at the gates of Florence, but this almost miraculous escape only postponed the day of reckoning. A vast migration of Goths, Huns, Vandals, Alans and other tribes was taking place and on December 31st, 406 a mass crossing of the frozen Rhine near Mainz could not be prevented. The great city of Trier was destroyed and the invaders overran France, reaching the British Channel in the north, the Mediterranean Sea in the south and the Atlantic Ocean in the west. The legions stationed in Britain had to be withdrawn to defend the homeland.

Then Stilicho, himself a Vandal, fell under suspicion of being in league with the enemy and was executed at Ravenna, which henceforth became the residence of the Emperor Honorius in preference to both Rome and Milan. Stilicho's place was taken by a lawyer to whom Augustine wrote urging him to use his high office for the good of the Catholic Church and to make sure everyone understood that the laws promulgated against idolatry and heretics during Stilicho's lifetime had emanated from the Emperor himself and were thus still in force. The intensification of the struggle between Catholics and Donatists in Africa resulted in several bishops travelling to Ravenna to enlist imperial support in a situation which looked like degenerating into civil war. The visitors brought back very disturbing reports of the state of the Empire, whose traditional boundaries on the Danube and the Rhine had long ceased to be secure. Hordes of desperate warriors were spreading fire and slaughter throughout western Europe. The scale of these events began to raise new intellectual problems for those who had time to think. Why were the servants of God cut off just as much as wicked men? Why were Christian women subjected to rape? Why should these awful things be happening to society at a time when Christianity was triumphant throughout the Empire? Had not conditions been more secure in the old days when the pagan gods were worshipped and the temples were full?

Pondering these questions did not distract Augustine from more immediate duties. A man named Faventius, a tenant on the Paratian Forest Estate, got into some trouble with the owner. Hoping that Augustine would mediate on his behalf, he took refuge in the church at Hippo. Nobody interfered with him there, so after several days he decided it was all right to go and have supper at a friend's house. However, he was being watched and on leaving the house he was arrested by an officer with a band of men. Someone reported his abduction to Augustine. As he was not sure who was responsible for it, Augustine appealed to the commander of the coastguards who sent out a search party of soldiers but without success. Next day Augustine found out where Faventius had been held overnight and tried to contact him. But the prisoner had been moved on at dawn and when Augustine's agent caught up with his captors he was not allowed to see him. Hearing this, Augustine wrote an official letter asking for the observance of the imperial ruling which allowed such a person thirty days on bail before trial. If a quick trial took place he was afraid the estate owner's great wealth might result in a miscarriage of justice. He also went to see the magistrate in charge, appealing to him to deal with the matter in an honourable and Christian manner. We do not know what happened.

Then one day early in 410 Augustine was approached by

a Greek-speaking student of rhetoric at Carthage named Dioscorus, who wanted immediate answers to a string of questions about the Dialogues of Cicero. The boy wrote impatiently because his brother had secured him a free travel pass and he was on the point of leaving to visit his parents in Greece. He had hoped to get help from Alypius but discovered he was away on a trip to Mauretania. Knowing of Augustine's former eminence in classical studies he boldly sent a messenger with several pages of questions and a covering letter. 'What I require is not money,' he assured the bishop, 'and you can easily grant this request of mine simply by speaking.'

At first Augustine was not at all pleased. 'When I consider how a bishop is distracted by the cares of his office clamouring on every side, it does not seem to me proper for him suddenly, as if deaf, to withdraw from all these and devote himself to expounding to a single student some unimportant questions in the Dialogues of Cicero.' He was amazed that anyone should write from a cultural centre like Carthage to enquire on such a subject at Hippo, where he did not even know how to lay hands on manuscripts of Cicero's works. In his indignation he let slip the information that his hair was going white. But although he protested at the large number of questions the boy had asked, they awakened such memories that in addition to making marginal notes on the question sheets, he dictated a thirty-page reply. He was able to do this because he was ill when the messenger arrived and during his convalescence away from Hippo he was unusually free to give his mind to such matters. He had never forgotten how much he owed to Cicero, whose learning and unique mastery of words he was still able to admire.

He also took the opportunity to tell Dioscorus that 'in our day no error dares to rally round it the uninstructed crowd without seeking the shelter of the Christian name.' In his experience the older Greek teachers posed no great threat to the gospel message. He felt that Plato had come much nearer to the truth than other philosophers and he knew many Christians who had great affection for him because of the charm of his style and the accuracy of many of his insights. 'With the intuition of genius he observed the invisible realities of God' to some extent, though still a long way from full understanding. 'The Stoic and Epicurean philosophies were more recent but even their ashes are not so warm that a single spark can be struck from them against the Christian faith. The din which resounds in the battle-fields of controversy comes now from innumerable small companies of sectaries, some of them easily discomforted, others presuming to make bold resistance, such as the partisans of Donatus and Mani here, or the unruly herds of Arians, Eunomians, Macedonians, Cataphrygians and other pests which abound in the countries to which you are going.' Along with all this he pointed Dioscorus to Jesus Christ, the way and the truth. 'In that way the first part is humility. This I would continue to repeat as often as you might ask direction, not that there are no other instructions which may be given but because, unless humility precede, accompany and follow every good action which we perform pride wrests wholly from our hand any good work on which we are congratulating ourselves. All other vices are to be apprehended when we are doing wrong, but pride is to be feared even when we do right.'

In his weakness he found it hard to endure the cold and heavy rain which afflicted North Africa during the 'exceptionally dreadful winter' in the early months of 410. He had to stay away from Hippo so long that his congregation rather lost patience with him and suspended the custom of providing clothes for the poor which, under his influence, they had maintained for many years. He attributed it partly to moral sloth in reaction to the reports from Europe of calamities so shocking that they seemed to be the fulfilment of what Christ had predicted would precede the end of the world. He wrote to remind them that it was only his poor health which had exempted him from the duty of travel overseas undertaken by some of his colleagues.

With the coming of kinder weather he recovered his strength and was back at his post by the day which signalled a momentous change in the history of the western world.

Chapter Twenty-One

THE ROMAN REFUGEES

On the night of August 24th, 410 Rome fell to the forces of
Alaric the Goth. After eight hundred years of imperial
supremacy, the eternal city was given up to several days of
carnage, burning and looting by the victorious soldiers from
eastern Europe. However, the Goths had previously adopted
Christianity in its Arian form, so they respected churches and
spared the lives of many who sought sanctuary in them.
Honorius remained powerless at Ravenna, secure behind the
marshes near the mouth of the River Po.

Knowing that Rome's million inhabitants had been sup-
plied with grain from Africa, Alaric planned to take his
people over to Carthage, searching for a land where he could
settle them in safety. His army moved down into the toe of
Italy where, across a few miles of water, the mountains of
Sicily loomed like a huge stepping stone bisecting the Mediterranean. Africa trembled at what was to come, but Alaric's
transports were wrecked in a storm, the invasion plan had to
be dropped, and his army turned back from what had proved
to be a cul-de-sac. That same autumn of 410 he died. His
men diverted a river, buried him in its bed, brought the river
back over his grave, and massacred all the prisoners who had
done the work and knew where the great commander lay.
Thus the Gothic battering ram lost its driving power. Meanwhile the Atlantic wing of the barbarian invasion surged over
the Pyrenees and spread havoc through Spain. The Vandals,
who had started from their base in Hungary, eventually
settled in the mountains behind Gibraltar where the region
of Andalusia still suggests their name.

Africa was invaded not by the Goths but by Roman refugees. Those who got away before or after the fall of Rome were mostly people who could afford the price of liberty. One wealthy Roman lady named Albina, together with her daughter Melania and son-in-law Pinianus, spent two years in Sicily and then settled at Tagaste to the great satisfaction of Alypius and the Church there. However, the arrival of such affluent Christians in Numidia was a disturbing event, for it was rumoured that Pinianus gave money away freely. The outcome was that when he visited Hippo the people seized him, as they had once seized Augustine, and demanded that the bishop ordain him on the spot. Alypius was also present and the two friends suddenly found themselves faced with an ugly situation in church. An angry clamour broke out against Alypius, who was judged not to favour their plans. Augustine was forced to tell the disorderly mob that if they compelled him to ordain Pinianus against the latter's will he would refuse to continue as their bishop. He then sat down and some senior men rallied round him, but the crowd massed below the steps was shouting at Alypius and threatening violence. Augustine wondered if he dared try escorting Alypius out of the building but feared they might not get through. They were at their wits' end when Pinianus sent a man in to say that if he was forcibly ordained he would leave Africa altogether. Hesitating to announce this, Augustine went out to him, taking the risk of leaving Alypius alone. Pinianus promised he would remain in Hippo so long as he was not ordained against his will. This brought immediate relief to Augustine and he quickly told Alypius, who could only say, 'Let no one ask my opinion on this subject.' Augustine then called for silence and told the people what Pinianus had proposed. The leaders consulted in undertones and then asked Pinianus to promise in addition that if he ever did get ordained it would be in Hippo. Pinianus agreed and when Augustine announced this the crowd was overjoyed, demanding that an oath be taken at once.

Pinianus then realised that under certain circumstances he

might need to to leave Hippo, particularly if the barbarians invaded Africa. Augustine feared that if any exception was made the people would suspect they were being deceived, but they decided to try it. Pinianus dictated a clause allowing him to leave in case of invasion, but there was an immediate outcry and he had to order it to be struck out. Although Augustine was exhausted by the strain of such a struggle, Pinianus insisted they go back into the church together. The double promise was read out and he assured everyone that he had confirmed it by an oath. They cried out 'Thanks be to God' and called for his signature on the spot. He signed before them all. Then the leaders asked Augustine and Alypius to sign too. As Augustine began to do so, Melania protested. Surprised that she did this so late, Augustine stopped. 'My signature remained incomplete and no one thought it necessary to insist further.'

It had been a nerve-racking experience, but the people of Hippo were delighted to have anchored such rich people in their community—until they discovered that Pinianus had left town the following day. It then fell to Augustine to pour oil on troubled waters, to make sure Pinianus returned, to calm the offended people of Tagaste, to retain the friendship of Alypius, and to soothe the feelings of Albina, the equally wealthy mother-in-law. This was a difficult task, for the general opinion in Tagaste was that Hippo was simply after the refugees' money. Moreover Albina, Pinianus and Melania all came to believe that Augustine himself had been motivated by covetousness and that he was responsible for ordering Pinianus to take such an oath. This damaging insinuation caused him great distress, for he had long ago given to the church at Tagaste his own family property there, 'which consisted of only a few small fields', though he ruefully admitted this could scarcely be considered 'a twentieth part of the ecclesiastical property which I am now supposed to possess'. He tried to enlist the help of Alypius in ridding the distinguished family of their suspicions, but once back in

Tagaste Alypius was not really on Augustine's side. Indeed both Alypius and Albina suggested to him that an oath extracted by force was invalid, but Augustine was not prepared to agree that perjury might occasionally be lawful for a Christian. He was dismayed that any responsible person should counsel Pinianus to break his oath, calling upon him to 'fulfil the promise by which he bound himself not to depart from Hippo, just as I myself and the other inhabitants of the town do not depart from it, having of course full freedom in going and returning at any time.'

Vows and signatures notwithstanding, nothing more is known about Pinianus and his family in Africa. Nine years later Jerome conveyed their greetings to Augustine from Bethlehem.

Chapter Twenty-Two

A TIME TO REFRAIN FROM EMBRACING

Quite a sensation was created in Carthage by the arrival of another family of very wealthy refugees headed by a widow named Proba whose sons had held high office in Rome. Having survived the fall of the city and then escaped from Italy while Alaric's army was in the south of the country, she reached Africa safely along with her daughter-in-law Juliana, also widowed, and Juliana's daughter Demetrias. Many other widows and girls travelled with these refined ladies. On reaching Carthage Proba was compelled to part with a considerable percentage of her fortune in favour of Heraclian, the Count of Africa, before he would allow her company to settle in the city.

In due course Proba wrote to Augustine, asking his advice about prayer. An interchange of letters followed and on his frequent visits to Carthage the ladies heard him preach. As a result, although arrangements for the marriage of Demetrias had already been completed, she decided to take a vow of chastity and become a nun, receiving the veil from Bishop Aurelius. Augustine and Alypius wrote her a joint letter to express their satisfaction and give her their advice. The family also requested Jerome to counsel the girl, which he did in a long letter from Bethlehem.

Ever since his conversion Augustine had held aloof from personal relationships with women. None were allowed to enter the monastery where he lived, not even his own widowed sister or the daughters of his uncle or his brother Navigius. In spite of this rigorous segregation and the sad experiences of his youth, Augustine's work as pastor and magistrate had given him wide knowledge of other people's struggles. Thus equipped, he wrote a series of books on marriage, celibacy and widowhood, expounding the biblical statements on such matters but also reflecting the strong prejudice of the age in favour of celibacy.

In one sense Augustine had a very high estimate of marriage. 'God instituted marriage from the beginning, before man's fall.' He approved marriage for life to one person only and was opposed to fornication before marriage, to adultery after it, and to divorce. Death alone terminated marriage, so that if a couple separated 'they continue wedded persons even after separation' and would be guilty of adultery if either remarried. On the death of a partner he allowed remarriage, refusing to condemn even a third or fourth marriage after bereavements. But this acknowledgement of the validity of the married state was modified by his insistence that sexual intercourse between husband and wife should be limited to what was absolutely necessary for the birth of children. In that he saw no fault, but he considered any further physical relations essentially faulty, requiring God's pardon, for they 'no longer followed reason, but lust', though he was prepared to grant that some good came out of the evil because people were thereby restrained from the deadly sin of adultery. This conviction was not weakened by his confession that in conversation with Christian couples he had never found any who had succeeded in limiting their relationship in this way.

In another sense Augustine had a low estimate of marriage because he so constantly and emphatically preferred celibacy. 'The weaker brothers in the married state, who have children or hope to have them' he contrasted with 'those who have a higher standard of life, who are not entangled with the bonds of matrimony'. When interpreting Christ's parable of the sower he inclined to identify those who bore fruit thirty-fold with married Christians, those who bore fruit sixty-fold with widows who refrained from marrying again, and those who bore fruit a hundred-fold with the celibate, 'virgins, holy boys and girls, trained up in the Church'. Times without number he reiterated that while marriage is good, to avoid it is better, much better. 'The virginity of your child,' he assured Juliana, 'has compensated for the loss of your virginity. Coming after you in birth, she has risen above you in honour and gone before you in holiness.' He anticipated that in heaven there would be special joy and rewards for the virgins of Christ, such as would not be experienced by the rest of the faithful. 'The others are below in work and wages.' He never ceased to advocate, in preference to matrimony, the holier, spiritual marriage to Christ, 'the Spouse of virgins'.

With Faustus' diatribe against the morals of the Jewish patriarchs never far from his mind, he returned again and again to their defence, arming himself with the verse which says there is 'a time to embrace and a time to refrain from embracing' (Ecclesiastes 3:5). With passionate oratory he explained that the Old Testament era was the time to embrace, for it was essential that the people of God should multiply as a preparation for the gospel and that prophets of Christ's coming might arise among them. Indeed he suggested that the whole Jewish race was then 'nothing else but a Prophet of Christ' and that for this reason righteous men were allowed more than one wife, not because they were overcome by lust but because they were 'led by piety'. He insisted that the patriarchs had physical relations with their wives solely for the purpose of having children. 'They felt no unlawful lust for any of them.' Such married life he held to be prophetic, God's deep plan lying hidden in it, so that it was a matter of obedience to God. In one of the most dramatic passages in all his writings he looked forward to sitting down with all true believers in the kingdom of heaven along with Abraham, Isaac and Jacob who 'for the sake of Christ were husbands, for the sake of Christ were fathers'.

In contrast, Augustine viewed the age in which he himself lived as the time to refrain from embracing. The people of

God had become numerous in many nations. There was no further need to serve Christ's coming by having children. Now that He had come, He was better served by restraint. No duty to mankind required marriage to be undertaken. Only those who could not otherwise control themselves should embark upon it, for it had become no more than a remedy for human weakness. To the objection that the continuance of the race would be jeopardised if everyone took his advice, Augustine's answer was that he was much more interested in completing the number of saints and thus hastening the end of the world.

So he did his best to discourage Juliana from contemplating a second marriage, though in writing to her he was also thinking of others who would learn of his words, such as one girl who had been twice widowed in two years and an older woman whose husband had gone abroad soon after their marriage and never come back. Although Juliana had had several sons as well as Demetrias, her husband had died comparatively young and he urged Proba to pray for her since she was still at a dangerous age. 'Ruth is blessed,' he told her, 'but Anna is more blessed.' He presumed she would not descend to the use of make-up, white or red, and he warned her and Demetrias not to become proud of their abstinence and to beware lest the desire for money replaced the desire for marriage. He regretted that he had known many virgins who had become talkative, drunken, covetous and proud, so he counselled his readers against wandering eyes, unbridled tongues, petulant laughs, scurrilous jests, against 'bosses of hair swelling out and coverings so yielding that the fine network below appears'. Believing obedience to be the mother of all virtues, he went so far as to state that 'a more obedient married woman is to be preferred to a less obedient virgin'. But, having said that, he advised the ladies to turn their backs on the delights of matrimony and devote themselves instead to reading and prayer, to singing psalms and meditating on the law of God, to frequent good works and hopes of the world to come, to gazing on the beauty of Christ, remembering His blood and the price He paid for their redemption. 'Whatever love you had to expend upon your marriages, pay back to Him.'

In view of these convictions it is not surprising that Augustine had a profound respect for the Virgin Mary. He did not regard her as a sinner and he believed she remained a virgin throughout life. But in his time she had no place in popular devotion, there were no lady chapels, and no one addressed prayers to Mary. In fact, except when he was speaking about the birth of Christ, Augustine hardly ever mentioned her.

PART FIVE

411–420

YEARS OF TRIUMPH AND TRAGEDY

Chapter Twenty-three

THE RISE OF PELAGIUS

Meanwhile a humbler but historically more important refugee had reached the coast of Africa. Pelagius, a layman some years younger than Augustine, a gifted teacher of the Christian faith, came originally from Britain. He had lived for many years in Rome, where he wrote books on the Trinity, on some New Testament Epistles, and on Christian morality. His fellow countryman Coelestius shared his concern at the moral laxity prevalent among Christians after a hundred years of imperial favour. Both men came to feel that the emphasis laid by the Church on the doctrine of original sin, on the weakness of human nature, and on the absolute necessity for the grace of God, encouraged moral inertia by making people think they neither could nor need do anything themselves, being mere puppets in the hands of their Creator.

In this frame of mind Pelagius studied Augustine's *Confessions* and was not pleased by his repetition of the prayer, 'Grant what You command and command what You will.' When these words were quoted in his presence by a bishop he excitedly contradicted them because they attributed everything in the Christian life to God. News of the incident got back to the bishop of Hippo. 'I first became acquainted with Pelagius' name, along with great praise of him, at a distance, when he was living in Rome. Afterwards reports began to reach us that he disputed against the grace of God.' Augustine realised he ought to listen to this new voice. 'In the last few days I have read some writings by Pelagius, a holy man as I am told, who has made no small progress in the Christian life.'

At this point Pelagius' campaign for moral reformation

was rudely disturbed by Alaric's advance on Rome. He and Coelestius got away to Sicily and eventually to Numidia, probably during Augustine's illness. 'On his arrival in Africa he was in my absence kindly received on our coast of Hippo.' However, Pelagius did not stay long. When Augustine got back to the city he enquired whether the visitor had said anything against the grace of God and learnt that 'nothing whatever of this kind was heard from him'. Later on, in Carthage, 'I caught a glimpse of him, once or twice to the best of my recollection, when I was very much occupied preparing for a conference we were to hold with the Donatists.' This was the only occasion they met and by the time Augustine was free to pay attention to him, Pelagius had left for Jerusalem, never to return to Africa. 'Meanwhile the doctrines connected with his name were warmly maintained and passed from mouth to mouth among his reputed followers.'

So far was Pelagius from nourishing any personal ill will towards Augustine that he wrote to him expressing 'many good and kind wishes'. Now that the chance had gone Augustine found himself 'greatly longing to have a conversation with him in person', so he replied briefly but cordially. 'I thank you very much for the pleasure you have afforded me by your letter. May the Lord requite you with blessings, may you ever enjoy them and live with Him for evermore in all eternity, my most beloved lord and most longed for brother.' And he added, 'Pray for me that the Lord would make me such a man as you suppose me to be already.'

With Pelagius far away, calling on Jerome at Bethlehem, Augustine might not have been further involved with his views had not Coelestius been so outspoken that a council of bishops was convened to consider his opinions. Coelestius was condemned and shortly afterwards left Africa, but the issues that had been raised began to attract widespread attention throughout the Christianised Roman world.

Although he himself had no wish to oppose the Catholic Church or question the authority of the Bible, Pelagius' teaching did constitute a reconsideration of accepted views about the fall of man and the doctrine of original sin transmitted from Adam to the entire human race. Coelestius' saying that 'Adam's sin injured only Adam himself' epitomised this attitude. In his study of the New Testament Pelagius had been struck by the emphasis laid on the force of example, the example of Christ, the example of Paul, the example of Timothy. He maintained that we are all born in a morally neutral state, without virtue and without vice. Adam sinned by his own choice. His descendants sin in the same way, not because they are programmed to do so, but by following his bad example. Sin, he insisted, 'is not born with us but done by us'. He could not tolerate the idea that God, who forgives sin, actually imputes Adam's sin to us when we are in a state of uncomprehending innocence.

Human beings at birth he regarded as in the same condition as Adam before he disobeyed God, free to choose good or evil. He insisted that the fall of Adam has no more automatic effect on others than does the resurrection of Christ : what Christ did is only effective for the man who makes it his own by faith; what Adam did is only damaging for the man who makes it his own by imitation. This led Pelagius to deny that original sin was a punishable offence. He felt it was monstrous to suggest that infants who died unbaptised would perish. Like Jerome, he believed that each soul was newly created by God, not derived from parents along with the body, so he did not regard sin as an inherited infection but as something each individual either did or did not choose to do. Thus, though he was as aware as Augustine of the wickedness of contemporary society, he denied that this depravity was transmitted from the first man or that infants were damned, unless in due course they themselves chose to do evil. He considered that human nature has the capacity not to sin. 'We contradict the Lord to His face when we say, "It is hard, we cannot do it, we are only men, encompassed with fragile flesh." O blind madness! We charge the God of all knowledge with a twofold ignorance : that He does not seem to know what He has made, nor what He has commanded.'

None of this meant that Pelagius was a humanist who turned his back on the revelation of God in the Bible or that he was obsessed with the ability of man to improve himself. He remained an ardent Christian, claiming absolute orthodoxy, seeking to understand and apply all aspects of New Testament teaching, believing that 'the grace of God, whereby Christ Jesus came into the world to save sinners, is necessary not only for every hour and every moment but also for every act of our lives', as Pinianus and Melania assured Augustine they had themselves heard him say. However, he used the phrase 'the grace of Christ' in an inclusive sense to allude to much more than the sacrifice of Christ on the cross, which he seems not to have specially emphasised. To him God's grace embraced His endowment of mankind with free will, the law of Moses, the forgiveness of sins through the death of Christ, the example of Christ and the teaching of Christ. 'The grace by which we conquer,' he used to say, 'has offered us teaching and example.' Such views inclined him to employ allegory sparingly, to make more use of the New Testament than the Old, and to underline the moral aspects of Christ's teaching recorded in the Gospels as a corrective to the contemporary tendency to exalt doctrinal orthodoxy above everything else. He wanted to maintain the reasonable balance he found in the New Testament between God's work and man's response, without denigrating either. Convinced that the capacity for right thinking, speaking and acting is God's gift to mankind, he was equally convinced that it is we ourselves who actually choose to think, speak and act righteously. He had little to say about the Christian's need to be strengthened by the Holy Spirit in order to obey the word of God, but his personality and his attractiveness as a teacher were such that, although he founded no separate church, what came to be called Pelagianism was soon in evidence all over the Roman Empire. 'Let us ponder these things day and night, my friends', he said. 'It is a great thing to be a son of God, to possess eternal life in all its richness and to have the prospect of the joys of reigning with God in heaven. Let us then strive with all the powers at our command to overcome our habits of sin and dip ourselves deep in activities of holiness and righteousness, that we may not undergo the sufferings of the damned but enjoy the blessed state together with the righteous.'

Emphasising in this way the part played by man's free will, Pelagius found himself in diametrical opposition to the idea that by God's inscrutable decree a limited number were chosen for salvation while the majority of mankind were condemned to be lost. In his opinion this made nonsense of God's clearly expressed desire that all men should be saved. Such a text as Romans 9 : 18, 'God has mercy on whom He wants to have mercy, and He hardens whom He wants to harden', was particularly difficult for him to accept. He decided the statement must be a gloss inserted by an opponent of the gospel, for he was convinced it was only the devil who hardened men's hearts. Struggling to interpret the Scriptures correctly, while avoiding monstrous assertions about God, he came to identify predestination with foreknowledge. He taught that God does not will the damnation of anyone : men condemn themselves by rejecting God's love; predestination is simply that God foreknows this, knows it before it happens; it is only a chronological accident that His foreknowledge precedes the event, for it does not determine it, but rather vice versa.

The strongest evidence for the effectiveness of his appeal was that before long Augustine embarked upon a tremendous series of books and booklets designed to refute the arguments of the layman from Britain.

Chapter Twenty-Four

THE CONFERENCE AND THE SCEPTICS

Soon after Rome had fallen to the Goths, the Emperor Honorius, still secure at Ravenna, sent to Africa a special representative name Marcellinus, charged with the task of putting an end to the Donatist problem. Marcellinus was a Catholic, a correspondent of Jerome's, and soon on intimate terms with Augustine. In June 411 he summoned both parties to a conference at Carthage which was attended by no fewer than 570 bishops, 286 of them Catholic and 284 Donatist. It was not really a conference at all but a grim confrontation in order to pronounce formal condemnation on the Donatist Church. Not to have accepted the invitation to attend would merely have deprived Donatists of the chance to speak in their own defence. 'By imperial commands we compelled them to meet with us,' said Augustine. Each side was allowed seven official spokesmen, seven advisors to them, and four secretaries to supervise the drawing up of a record of the proceedings. Augustine, Alypius and Possidius were among the Catholic spokesmen. Petilian was the most prominent leader among the Donatists, so Augustine at last saw and heard him in person.

A century of strife meant that there was no love lost between the parties. At one session the Donatists, quoting Psalm 26 :4, refused to sit down with 'false men', so every one had to remain standing. June 1st and June 3rd were spent in stormy argument; then the crisis came when, after several days without convening, the final sessions were held on June 8th. At this stage Augustine played a leading part, though Petilian tried to discredit him by reminding the assembly that Megalius, the Catholic primate of Numidia, had once had reservations about consecrating him bishop.

The conflict continued from first light to long after dark, and it was by candlelight that Marcellinus pronounced his inevitable verdict in favour of the Catholic Church. He had done his best to conduct the debate fairly, though he was a blatantly prejudiced chairman. The Donatists were also convinced he had been bribed. They appealed at once to the Emperor, but there was no help for them in that quarter and they soon found they had become an illegal, criminal organisation. Unless they agreed to become Catholic as entire communities, their church buildings had to be surrendered. Their bishops and clergy were fined and all Donatist property was, 'through the religious laws of our Christian emperors' as Augustine put it, confiscated and given to the Catholic Church. In succeeding years those who remained obstinate lost all civil rights, were turned out of the towns in which they lived, and in some cases deported to remote parts of the sprawling Empire.

Thanks to such violent measures, the menace of the Circumcellions to the Romanised population and the challenge of the Donatist Church to ecclesiastical unity ceased to be significant. When all allowance has been made for the Emperor's anxiety to achieve a united Africa at a time of all-out war, it has to be admitted that Augustine lent his great authority to cruel proceedings, carried out in the name of Christian love, which set a disastrous precedent for subsequent generations. The strength of Christianity among the African peasants and intellectuals lay in the Donatist Church. It can be argued that by invoking the power of the state to eradicate Donatism by legal, financial and military pressures he did more damage to the worldwide cause of the Christian Church than all the benefits conferred upon it by the genius of his personality and teaching.

Meanwhile Marcellinus and Augustine were drawn together in mutual admiration and friendship by the struggle in which they had played such significant roles. Augustine even admired his friend's family life, though he was not above suggesting that Marcellinus 'would have relinquished all secular business and girded himself with the insignia of the Christian warfare had he not been prevented by having entered into the married state.' In Carthage Marcellinus was in touch with a circle of cultured Romans who used to meet in the evenings for friendly discussion. Among them was a man named Volusianus, whose mother was concerned about him and had persuaded Marcellinus to visit him daily. Augustine knew her and admired the way she prayed for her son as Monica had for him. Volusianus was already in touch with the bishop by letter. In his reply, remembering how difficult he had once found the prophecy of Isaiah, Augustine advised him to 'read the writings of the apostles, for from them you will receive a stimulus to acquaint yourself with the prophets, whose testimonies the apostles use'.

He encouraged him to write again if any difficult questions arose in the course of his study and it was not long before Volusianus did so. On some occasion when the group of friends had been discussing poetry and philosophy for a long time, one of the company boldly confessed he had grave doubts about the truth of Christianity and found the virgin birth of Christ incredible. He questioned very much whether the ruler of the whole world could possibly have become an insignificant infant and suggested the miracles recorded in the Gospels could be paralleled elsewhere and were in any case 'but small works for God to do'. At this the others prevented him from saying anything more and the meeting broke up.

Then, recalling Augustine's offer of help, Volusianus wrote to him. 'Ignorance may, without harm to religion, be tolerated in other priests,' he affirmed, 'but when we come to Bishop Augustine, whatever we find unknown to him is no part of the Christian system.' As was his custom, Augustine rejected any suggestion that he was infallible. 'Such is the depth of the Christian Scriptures,' he replied, 'that even if I were attempting to study them and nothing else from early boyhood to decrepit old age with the utmost leisure, the most unwearied zeal, and talents greater than I have, I would still be daily making progress in discovering their treasures.' Busy as he was with all the work involved in the leadership of his community, in preaching and counselling as well as writing several books simultaneously, he still managed to find time for an extended reply, postponing other matters which he had intended dictating to his secretaries.

Meanwhile Marcellinus confided in Augustine that the group were troubled by many other problems about Christianity. They were perplexed because the God of the New Testament was said to have abrogated what He had commanded in the Old Testament, thus laying Himself open to the charge of inconsistency. Furthermore, they felt that Christian teaching was incompatible with the duties of Roman citizens, specially because it advocated turning the other cheek and not recompensing evil for evil, precepts which could hardly be applied at a time when the Empire was being attacked by barbarian invaders. Then there was the worrying fact that such great disasters should have occurred when the emperors professed to be Christians.

Augustine sent his reply to Marcellinus alone, leaving it to him to use his discretion in sharing it with the others. With regard to the change from 'the comparative darkness of the Old Testament,' he asked, 'Does not summer follow winter, the temperature gradually increasing in warmth? How often our own lives experience changes. Boyhood departing, never to return, gives place to youth; manhood, destined itself to continue only for a season, takes in turn the place of youth; and old age, closing the term of manhood, is itself closed by death. All these things are changed, but the plan of divine providence which appoints these successive changes is not changed.'

He suggested that the commands in the Sermon on the Mount ought not to be taken too literally, since neither Christ nor Paul actually turned the other cheek when struck, but rather protested, suggesting that such verses relate to a Christian's attitude, not to his precise actions. Then he appealed directly to the group. 'Let those who say that the doctrine of Christ is incompatible with the state's wellbeing give us an army composed of soldiers such as the doctrine of Christ requires them to be : let them give us such subjects, such husbands and wives, such parents and children, such masters and servants, such kings, such judges, such taxpayers and tax gatherers as the Christian religion has taught that men should be, and then let them dare to say that it is adverse to the state's wellbeing. Rather, let them confess that this doctrine, if it were obeyed, would be the salvation of the commonwealth.'

He had no difficulty in quoting from the historian Sallust and the poet Juvenal to prove that the downfall of the Romans began long before there were any Christian emperors and that in past centuries prosperity led to unlimited wickedness, when 'dire corruption, more terrible than any invader, took possession of the mind of the state.' In such circumstances he unashamedly regarded the cross of Christ as a wonderful deliverance from the vile abyss of depravity into which men were helplessly sinking.

This exchange of letters with Marcellinus was of more than passing significance, for in his reply Augustine had begun to grapple with the issues which he was to elaborate over the next fifteen years in his book, *The City of God*, which is in wide circulation to this day. Its opening sentence is, 'Here, my dear Marcellinus, is the fulfilment of my promise.'

Chapter Twenty-Five

THE FALL OF THE MIGHTY

Violence occurred in the wake of the condemnation of Donatism at the Carthage Conference and the harsh laws subsequently passed against it. The great majority of the victims
were Donatists, but two Catholic priests also suffered : one
was killed, the other lost an eye and a finger. Those held to
be responsible were arrested and brought to trial before
Marcellinus, who had them beaten during the interrogation.
Since torture was normal for underprivileged people, Augustine congratulated him on his mildness in not requiring the
gaolers to stretch them on the rack, furrow their flesh with
iron claws or scorch them with flames, as he might well have
done. But he was still afraid the men would be executed or
maimed in the way they were accused of maiming others.
So, appealing to Marcellinus as a friend and bishop, he counselled clemency. 'Let your indignation against their crimes
be tempered by considerations of humanity.' Not everyone
approved of such advice, regarding it as a sign of weakness
at a time when a Donatist bishop was going round the villages
trying to reopen their churches. But Augustine was not to be
outdone. Through Marcellinus he appealed to the Proconsul
not to inflict capital punishment and thus create further
martyrs on the Donatist side. If his advice was disregarded,
he let it be known he would appeal to the Emperor.

Meanwhile he was busy preparing a précis of the volumi-
nous proceedings of the Carthage Conference. 'If I could set
before you a statement of the toil which it is absolutely necessary for me to devote, by day and by night, to other duties,
you would deeply sympathise with me and would be aston-
ished at the amount of business which distracts my mind. I
have difficulty in obtaining even a very little leisure amidst
the accumulation of work into which, in spite of my inclina-

tions, I am dragged by other men's wishes or necessities, and what I am to do I really do not know.' Pressure was such that when Marcellinus returned some of his manuscripts he had to confess, 'I have forgotten for what reason I received them again from you.'

Marcellinus had staunchly defended opinions Augustine had expressed in his book on *Free Will*, but the bishop was quick to caution him. 'I endeavour to be one of those who write because they have made some progress and who, by means of writing, make further progress. If, in opposing those by whom I am censured, you maintain the position that I have nowhere in my writings made a mistake, you labour in a hopeless enterprise, you have undertaken a bad cause.' In fact he confided in his friend that one day he hoped to write a book collecting and reconsidering all those passages in his books with which he had subsequently become dissatisfied, a feat which he actually accomplished in old age.

Marcellinus knew that for years he had been working on a substantial volume on the book of Genesis and another on the Trinity. He urged the bishop to hurry up and publish them, but Augustine's philosophy of authorship was different. Experience with 'my other more hastily published works' had taught him that it was better to wait, revising what he had written again and again, so that 'those who are the judges, sternly impartial' would find nothing to censure. Sometimes he had reason to regret the way he had expressed himself in letters too. One of these so grieved a fellow bishop that Augustine tried to get a talk with him, but the man declined to come to Hippo. Augustine felt it better not to go to him 'that we might not make ourselves a laughing stock to those outside the pale of the Church'. So he enlisted a friend's help. 'I was too vehement and not sufficiently guarded. I entreat him to remember our old friendship and forget my recent offence. Let him exhibit in granting pardon the gentleness which I failed to show in writing that letter.'

During 413 one man's selfish ambition cost many lives in

Africa. Heraclian, who had personally executed Stilicho and subsequently become Count of Africa, tried to overthrow Honorius. He gathered a formidable flotilla at Carthage and sailed for Italy, where he was ignominiously defeated by a general named Marinus who was promptly appointed Count of Africa in his stead. Honorius at once sent Marinus to Carthage to punish those who had been implicated in the revolt. Fear gripped the city as informers tried to advance themselves by accusing others. Execution without proper trial all too easily followed baseless information laid by a single person. Many prominent people fled in terror to seek asylum in churches. Augustine was visiting Carthage at the time and so was an old friend of his, Caecilianus, Governor of Numidia, who was repeatedly seen in private consultation with Marinus.

To Augustine's amazement, one of those called in for questioning about Heraclian's affair was Marcellinus, along with his brother. Both were soon released but then, after Caecilianus had conferred with Marinus, rearrested. Some people deduced that there must be a Donatist influence behind this sequence of events, though Marinus allowed a Catholic bishop to leave for Ravenna to intercede for them at the imperial court. Anxious for the safety of his friend, Augustine succeeded in visiting him in prison. Fearing that he might have been unfaithful to his wife, 'since human nature is liable to fall into such wickedness', Augustine asked him if there was any sin for which he ought specially to seek reconciliation with God. Marcellinus blushed, thanked the bishop for his warning, and then 'seized my right hand with both his hands and said, "I swear by the sacraments which are dispensed to me by this hand that I have neither before nor since my marriage been guilty of immoral self-indulgence."'

Caecilianus called on Augustine to assure him that because of the friendship between himself and Marinus the two brothers would be all right. He was about to sail for Rome and said Marinus had made him a present of their lives before he left. He confirmed this by a solemn oath, stretching out his hand towards the church as he did so, but the very next day Augustine was dismayed to hear that they had been taken from the prison for trial before Marinus. The Governor's words were still so fresh in his mind, however, that he was totally unprepared for the sudden arrival of a messenger with the news that they had just been beheaded, not at the usual place of execution but right outside the courtroom on the public recreation ground. 'I left Carthage immediately and secretly.'

From the greater safety of Hippo he corresponded with Caecilianus about what he regarded as a monstrous abuse of power by Marinus, for it seemed that the Emperor had actually ordered the release of Marcellinus. Realising that the Governor had deceived him from start to finish, he wrote with infinite tact, never actually mentioning Marinus, and calling upon Caecilianus to clear his name from suspicion of having shared in a judicial murder. 'It will be interesting to us to learn by your Excellency's reply to this letter where you were on the day on which the crime was committed, how you received the news, and what you said to him when you next saw him.'

Caecilianus was suspiciously keen to induce Augustine to return to Carthage, but the bishop explained he was not well enough for that. 'In addition to my infirmities peculiar to myself which are known to all my more intimate friends, I am burdened with an infirmity common to the human family, the weakness of old age.' He was in fact fifty-nine. And he added a further good reason for avoiding Carthage. So far as he could find any leisure from his public duties as bishop, he was anxious to give the time to sacred studies, 'in doing which I may, if it please the mercy of God, be of some service even to future generations.'

Chapter Twenty-Six

THE REALLY DIFFICULT QUESTION

Evodius, though present at Monica's death, had not figured prominently in Augustine's life for many years. Like Alypius, he had spent some time in the monastery and he then became bishop of Uzala. A boy working in a solicitor's office was influenced by him and later employed as his secretary. When all was still at night he used to read aloud to Evodius and discuss with him anything hard to understand. Evodius found this rather a strain, yet admired the youth's zeal and moral discipline. When he was only twenty-two this boy fell seriously ill, lying for sixteen days in his father's house repeating Bible verses and singing psalms before he died. Evodius was deeply moved by his passing. 'For three days we continued to praise the Lord with hymns at his grave.' He wondered as never before just what happens to the soul after death and it seemed to him possible that it does take to itself some other kind of body. The fact that he had seen some of his dead friends in dreams encouraged him in the idea. So he tried it out on Augustine.

The bishop of Hippo wasted an hour looking in vain for a previous letter from Evodius and then confessed that he really did not have the time to devote to such a speculative matter. 'My opinion, however, if you are willing to hear it summed up in a sentence, is that I by no means believe that the soul departing from the body is accompanied by another body of any kind.' Convinced or not, Evodius reacted by asking Augustine's views on 'the spirits in prison' mentioned in 1 Peter 3 : 19. This time, since he too found the matter perplexing, he sent back a very thorough answer. Dissatisfied with the usual interpretation that Christ preached in hell to the people of Noah's time, passing over so many virtuous men of pre-Christian centuries, Augustine was inclined to think the passage did not refer to dead sinners at all but to living ones. He was unwilling to adopt the opinion that those who have not had an opportunity of hearing the gospel in this life may get it in the hereafter, for that would have implied the church was being built in hell as well as on earth and lessened the urgency of preaching to the living. Holding firmly to the clear teaching of other New Testament passages, he understood 'spirits in prison' to mean contemporary unbelievers, without any reference to the afterlife, the allusion to Noah's time being merely for the sake of comparison. He did not advance this opinion authoritatively but asked Evodius to enlighten him if a better explanation could be put forward.

In 415 a youth named Orosius from Portugal, 'a man of quick understanding, ready speech and burning zeal' turned up in Hippo, drawn by the fame of its bishop. 'Nor has his coming been altogether in vain,' Augustine told Jerome. 'In the first place he has learned not to believe all that report affirmed of me. In the next place, I have taught him all that I could. As for the things in which I could not teach him, I have told him from whom he may learn them and have exhorted him to go on to you.' It was an excellent chance to write to Jerome again, for Orosius had promised to call at Hippo with a reply on his way back. Although they had not communicated for some years and Jerome was now eighty-four, Augustine could never get the old man out of his mind, for at heart he knew that Jerome was his superior in pure biblical scholarship. 'My desire would be to have you daily beside me as one with whom I could converse on any theme.' So he composed two long letters, one on the origin of the soul, in which he could not resist a guarded attack on Jerome's view that God makes a new soul for each indivual at birth, and the other on the interpretation of James 2 : 10.

In the first of these letters Augustine asked Jerome's help in solving some intellectual problems to do with Christianity and children. He laid it down as beyond question that 'there is not one soul in the human family to whose salvation the one Mediator between God and men, the man Christ Jesus, is not absolutely necessary.' But in spite of all his 'praying, reading, thinking and reasoning', he was still not sure how to answer questions arising out of this conviction. Where had the soul of a newborn infant contracted the guilt from which it could only be rescued by 'the grace of the Mediator and the sacrament of that grace', baptism? 'Where is the justice of the condemnation of so many thousands of souls which, in the death of infant children, leave the world without the benefit of the Christian sacrament?'

He found even greater difficulty in accounting for the pain, deformity and imbecility with which he saw some children afflicted. 'Now God is good, God is just, God is omnipotent: let the great suffering which infants experience be accounted for by some reason compatible with justice.' He frankly confessed to Jerome his need for help in these matters. 'I cannot think that it is at any time in life too late to learn what we need to know.' He found some comfort in the story of the man who fell into a well where there was sufficient water to break his fall but not enough to drown him. A passer-by called down to him, 'How did you fall in there?' He replied, 'I beesech you, plan how you can get me out of this, rather than ask how I fell in.' But the theoretical problem continued to baffle him. 'I am embarrassed, believe me, by great difficulties and am wholly at a loss to find an answer.' He could not bring himself to evade 'the really difficult question', how a righteous God could justly condemn to eternal death an innumerable number of innocent, unbaptised infants. 'If you have either read, or heard from the lips of Jerome,' he begged another learned correspondent, 'or received from the Lord when meditating on this difficult question anything by which it can be solved, impart it to me, I beseech you.'

Augustine considered that a right understanding of James

2 : 10 was even more urgent and he regretted not having consulted Jerome about it before. This verse states that 'Whoever keeps the whole law but fails in one point has become guilty of all of it.' This perplexed him because of his conviction that no one is altogether without sin and that not all sins are equally bad. And he also asked, 'Has he no virtues who lacks one?' Wrestling with various possible solutions, he submitted it all to Jerome in what proved to be his last words to the old scholar. 'Do not hesitate to correct my error, for I pity the man who, in view of the unwearied labour and sacred character of your studies, does not render you the honour you deserve and give thanks to our Lord God by whose grace you are what you are.'

Orosius took the letters to Bethlehem and, true to his word, brought back Jerome's reply, though this proved to be little more than an acknowledgement. Jerome refused to argue any more with Augustine. 'For my part I am resolved to love you,' he said 'to look up to you, to reverence and admire you, and to defend your opinions as my own.' He contented himself with saying that Augustine had already stated 'whatever can be drawn by commanding genius from the fountain of sacred Scripture' on the themes in question. Hoping that he might yet receive a fuller answer, Augustine refrained from publishing his two letters till Jerome had died.

Meanwhile Orosius left for home but turned back from the island of Minorca on hearing of the devastation caused by the Vandals in Spain. Although Augustine was busily engaged in writing the eleventh book of *The City of God*, he again gave time to him and it was at his suggestion that Orosius began to write the *Seven Books of History against the Pagans*, which became a standard textbook in the Middle Ages, was translated into Anglo-Saxon by King Alfred, and is available in English to this day.

Chapter Twenty-Seven

THE ANSWER TO PELAGIUS

With Donatism officially proscribed, Augustine gave much of his time in the ten years which followed the Carthage Conference to the refutation of Pelagianism. His sermons, public discussions and letters were full of this theme and he also poured out a flood of treatises on the subject. Some of their titles indicate the scope of his counter-attack : *Original Sin, The Forgiveness of Sins, The Soul and its Origin, The Baptism of Infants, The Grace of Christ, Nature and Grace, Grace and Free Will.* It is remarkable that he managed to devote such detailed and sustained attention to an issue which, unlike Donatism, was not a major problem in Numidia itself.

To begin with Augustine spoke only cautiously against Pelagius. Having read one of his books, he commented 'I saw in it a man inflamed with most ardent zeal against those who, when in their sins they ought to censure human will, are more forward in accusing the nature of men, and thereby endeavour to excuse themselves. He shows too great a fire against this evil.' He was also anxious not to alienate unnecessarily 'certain of our brethren, most friendly and dear to us and without wilful guilt entangled in this error, but yet entangled.' Though increasingly anxious about Pelagius, he for some time retained a degree of respect and even affection for him, attacking his ideas without mentioning his name in order 'to preserve friendly relations with him and spare his personal feelings'. Lest he base his replies on unreliable evidence, he did his best to lay hands on all that Pelagius had written, sifting his books with the utmost care, marking passages which required fuller consideration, and quoting from them so extensively that he has preserved for us a great many of Pelagius' actual words.

Two of the latter's former disciples, amazed at Augustine's thoroughness and fairness in *Nature and Grace*, wrote to thank him for helping them perceive the error of the views they had adopted. The more he studied Pelagius' books the more his opinion hardened that the new emphasis constituted 'a poisonous perversion of the truth'. He sharply distinguished the issues Pelagius had raised from secondary matters on which divergent views were permissible, such as the location of the Garden of Eden or whether there was a fourth heaven as well as a third. Eventually he abandoned all restraint and openly attacked him as an enemy of the grace of God.

Alarmed at the degree of approval accorded to Pelagius by some bishops in the East, he released his avalanche of books, dictated day and night to an indefatigable staff of male secretaries. 'God's love "has been poured into our hearts",' he kept reiterating, 'not by free choice whose spring is in ourselves, but "through the Holy Spirit which has been given to us" (Romans 5 :5). Free choice, if the way of truth is hidden, avails for nothing but sin. The good life is a divine gift.'

Speaking of original sin, the most fundamental issue involved in the debate, he wholeheartedly endorsed Ambrose's statement, 'I fell in Adam : all of us are born in sin : our very origin is sin,' the only exception being Christ the Mediator, born of a virgin without the intervention of human desire. Though regretting that conception is 'impracticable without a certain amount of bestial motion which puts human nature to the blush', he did not blame marriage for the transmission of original sin but only human desire, which he never failed to call 'lust'. As a result he maintained that infants, though incapable of sinning, 'are not born without the contagion of sin, not because of what is lawful (meaning marriage) but on account of what is unseemly (meaning lust).' He argued that this universal birthstain could only be purged by baptism, the bath of regeneration, for nothing but the second birth could deliver from the bondage inherent in the first birth. On every newborn child his verdict was 'Eve's deceiver holds him, Mary's Son frees him.' The most he would concede was that 'the baptised infant fails to benefit from what he received as a little child, if on coming to years of reason, he fails to believe and to abstain from unlawful desires.'

While Augustine considered the fifth chapter of the Epistle to the Romans the complete answer to what he regarded as Pelagius' nebulous theory of the imitation of Adam, his prolonged studies in the book of Genesis also armed him for this struggle. Though well aware that some people regarded the whole creation story as a fable, he no more questioned the historicity of Adam and Eve than his opponent did. 'God chose to make a single individual the starting point for all mankind. This we believe on the authority of the Holy Scriptures. Anyone who is born anywhere as a man derives from that first human being, however extraordinary he may appear to us in shape, colour or utterance.' On one point, however, he himself remained entirely sceptical. 'If we did not know that monkeys, apes and chimpanzees are not men but animals, those who plume themselves on their collections of curiosities might pass them off on us as races of men and get away with such nonsense.'

He regarded the fall of Adam recorded in the third chapter of Genesis as 'a misuse of free will which started a chain of disaster, for we were all in that one man, seeing that we all were that one man'. Struggling to understand what it was that caused Adam to make the original wrong choice, since God had created him without sin, he came to the conclusion that this was 'like trying to see darkness or hear silence, so no one must try to get to know from me what I know that I do not know'. In asserting that men are born perverted, not morally neutral, he claimed to have the support of history and experience as well as Scripture. 'What else is the message of all the evils of humanity?' He drew up a catalogue of the hatred, treachery, cruelty, savagery, violence, lust and unnatural vice which darken every page of man's history. 'All these evils spring from that root of error which every son of Adam brings with him at his birth.'

Pelagius' views about predestination forced Augustine to review his own convictions, but not to change them. As long ago as 396 he had written to Simplicianus about the ninth chapter of the Epistle to the Romans, saying that 'unless the mercy of God in calling precedes, no one can even believe.' When challenged on this he had insisted that there could be no unrighteousness with God. 'His judgments are inscrutable and His ways past finding out. Let us sing Hallelujah and praise Him together in song.' The same problem arose when he was preaching on John 12 :38–40. 'When questions of this sort come before us, why this one is blinded by being forsaken by God and that one enlightened by divine aid, let us not take upon ourselves to pass judgment on the judgment of so mighty a judge.' Although occasionally admitting that 'this is too high for my stature and too strong for my strength,' he was not prepared to make any concessions to human sentiment. 'A deserved penalty is meted out to the damned, an undeserved grace to the saved; the former cannot complain that he is undeserving nor the latter boast that he is deserving.' So he felt no embarrassment in explaining Romans 9 :18, saying that God has mercy on some 'not through justice but by grace,' while He hardens others 'not through injustice but by the truth of retribution.' And these principles he then applied in the most uncompromising manner to newborn infants, insisting that none can enter the kingdom of heaven unless regenerated by baptism. 'One child, born in faithful wedlock, received with joy by its parents, but suffocated in sleep by mother or nurse, becomes an outcast with no share in its parents' faith. Another, born in shame and sacrilege, abandoned by the cruel fear of its mother but rescued by the compassionate charity of Christian strangers and baptised, becomes a partaker in the eternal kingdom.' Nothing would move him from this conviction that baptism was absolutely essential, irrespective of age. In his view the smallest infants would be judged by God according to what they had done 'when they believed or did not believe through the mouths and hearts of those who carried them when they were baptised or were not baptised.' In proof he pointed to Mark 16 : 16, 'Whoever believes and is baptised will be saved.' So he approved of the custom which had arisen in Carthage of calling baptism simply 'salvation'. When it was suggested to him that the thief on the cross was admitted to paradise unbaptised, he disagreed, saying that we rightly assume the baptism of many New Testament characters—including all the apostles except Paul—even though this is not actually recorded. The thief might have been baptised in prison or before he was arrested. There was even another possibility which occurred to Augustine. 'He might have been sprinkled with the water which gushed at the same time as the blood out of the Lord's side.'

Chapter Twenty-Eight
LOVE AND DO AS YOU LIKE

Some years earlier Augustine had embarked upon an ambitious series of 124 sermons in which he expounded the Gospel of John section by section. At Easter 415 he interrupted this to explain the First Epistle of John in ten sermons delivered in the course of only eight days. Occasionally he illumined the text by brief references to the experience of his hearers : to the carpenter considering what he could make out of a tree felled in the forest, to the ugly woman married to the handsome man, to the surgeon's knife enlarging the wound in order to heal it, to the needle passing through cloth so that the thread might follow, to the finger tapping a vase to see if it was cracked, to the cow patient with the calf butting her udders, to the riderless horse tossing its head and kicking its heels. Though he did not use a single story in illustration, he so held the attention of his audience day by day that at times they cried out in approval or were stirred to applause.

'I ask you today for your closest attention, since we have no light matter to consider,' he said as he came to 1 John 3 :9. 'Indeed the interest with which you listened to yesterday's sermon assures me that it will be even keener today. For the question to be raised is a very difficult one. We are asking what is meant by this text in our Epistle, 'No one who is born of God will continue to sin' in view of that earlier saying in the same Epistle, 'If we claim to be without sin, we deceive ourselves and the truth is not in us.' (1 John 1 :8). Now give your minds to these words. I want you to face the difficulty.'

With such an Epistle in front of him, Augustine laid his Easter emphasis upon God's love to us and the love to others which it demands from us. 'The words are not mine,' he declared. 'If it were I that said "God is love" any of you might take offence and say "What was that? What did he mean?" There, my brethren, is God's Scripture before you : this is a canonical epistle, read in every nation. Here you are told by the Spirit of God, "God is love" (1 John 4 :8). Now, if you dare, act against God and refuse to love your brother.'

He insisted that 'love is the only final distinction between the sons of God and the sons of the devil'. He roundly declared that anyone could be baptised, attend church, cross himself, receive the sacrament, answer Amen, sing Hallelujah, or utter prophecies, but love alone distinguished the true Christian from others, love alone was the special gift of the Spirit. 'At the church's beginning the Holy Spirit fell upon the believers and they spoke with tongues unlearnt,' he reminded them. 'It was a sign fitted to the time : all the world's tongues were a fitting signification of the Holy Spirit, because the gospel of God was to have its course through every tongue in all parts of the earth. The sign was given and then passed away. We no longer expect that those upon whom the hand is laid that they may receive the Holy Spirit will speak with tongues. When we laid our hand upon these "infants", the Church's newborn members, none of you (I think) looked to see if they would speak with tongues or, seeing that they did not, had the perversity to argue that they had not received the Holy Spirit. If then the Holy Spirit's presence is no longer testified by such marvels, on what is anyone to ground his assurance that he has received the Holy Spirit? Let him enquire of his own heart : if he loves his brother, the Spirit of God abides in him.'

'A short and simple precept is given you once for all,' he said in the seventh of these Easter talks, when he was explaining the definitive statement about the love of God in 1 John 4 :9. 'Love and do what you like. Whether you keep silence, keep silence in love; whether you exclaim, exclaim in love; whether you correct, correct in love; whether you forbear, forbear in love. Let love's root be within you and from that root nothing but good can spring. Who can do ill to any person whom he loves? Love, and you cannot but do well.' Torn from their context, his memorable words, 'Love and do what you like' have sometimes been used to justify immoral behaviour so long as it was accompanied by feelings of intense affection. Indeed, the idea misled Augustine himself. Identifying love with unity in subjection to the Catholic Church, he felt no Christian obligation to show what would normally be recognised as kindness, gentleness, or friendliness towards Donatists. So far as those outside the only Church he acknowledged were concerned, he persuaded himself that true love involved compelling them to conform.

In the village of Mutugenna, where he had once searched for a wayward deacon, there lived a Donatist leader whose own name was Donatus. Some months after delivering his course of Easter sermons Augustine ordered Donatus and another man to be arrested, brought to Hippo under guard, and put on trial, believing them to be responsible for many Catholics having left the Church. The second man submitted quietly, but Donatus refused to mount the horse Augustine had sent for him and instead tried to take his own life by dashing himself down headfirst on to rocky ground. This is not easy to do, and he was unsuccessful, but after reaching Hippo a second opportunity presented itself. He tried to drown himself by jumping into a well from which his captors managed to rescue him. He was then bold enough to protest to Augustine against his detention, arguing that God has given us free will and no one should be compelled to become a Catholic against his own judgment.

Augustine, however, insisted that compulsion to do good is permissible. Quoting 1 Timothy 3 : 1, 'If any one aspires to the office of bishop, he desires a noble task,' he pointed out that many had undertaken this noble task not because they wanted to but because they were physically compelled to do so. Paul, he asserted, was thrown to the ground and blinded so that he might be changed and become an apostle. He claimed it was his Christian duty to rescue Donatus from perishing in pernicious error by forcing him to accept salvation and enter the peace of the Church. Otherwise, 'being in a state of exclusion from the Church, severed from the body of unity and the bond of charity, you would be punished with eternal misery even though you were burned alive for Christ's sake.' He then proceeded to explain to the helpless prisoner, as he had done to Vincentius, his interpretation of Christ's parable of the great supper recorded in the fourteenth chapter of Luke's Gospel. 'The master of the house, after he had sent a message to the invited guests and they had refused to come, said to his servants, "Go out quickly to the streets and lanes of the city and bring in the poor and maimed and blind and lame." And the servant said, "Sir, what you commanded has been done, and still there is room." And the master said to the servant, "Go out to the highways and hedges and compel people to come in, that my house may be filled". Mark, now, how it was said in regard to those who came first, "bring them in"—it was not said "compel them to come in"—by which was signified the incipient condition of the Church when it was only growing towards the position in which it would have strength to compel men to come in. Accordingly, because it was right that when the Church had been strengthened, both in power and extent, men should be compelled to come to the feast of everlasting salvation, it was afterwards added in the parable "compel people to come in".' He had forgotten that he once said the exact opposite to the Donatist bishop Maximin at Mutugenna.

We do not know what happened to the prisoner, as there was no one to record the fate of such men, and for every ardent martyr spirit there were hundreds of Donatists who for personal and family reasons found it necessary to conform. So Augustine had no difficulty in finding men who thanked him warmly for forcing them to do so. But in the hinterland of south Numidia it was different, and even in coastal regions there were diehards still. A few years later

Augustine undertook the longest of all his African journeys, from Carthage right past Hippo to Caesarea, capital of Mauretania. As usual he recorded nothing of this trip through the mountains. One of his tasks at Caesarea was to dissuade the people from observing their ancestral custom of having an annual civil war which divided families into two factions fighting each other with stones for several days. Long afterwards he looked back with satisfaction to his success in stopping the bloodshed. But while he was there something else took place.

One day he chanced to meet in the street one of the Donatist spokesmen at the Carthage Conference, Emeritus, who had been their bishop in Caesarea for thirty years. Augustine promptly invited him into the Catholic church and he felt it wise to accept. A crowd assembled, to whom Augustine preached, asking them to pray for the conversion of Emeritus, who sat there in awkward silence, the centre of attention. Two days later a more formal meeting took place in the same building with several bishops present, including Alypius and Possidius, who wrote his own account of the proceedings.

'In the presence of people of different sects Augustine himself entered into discussion with Emeritus on their religious differences. It could not be said that he was not allowed to carry on the discussion with freedom or that in his own city and in the presence of his own followers he was denied the liberty to defend his doctrines. Nevertheless he declined to continue the discussion, though encouraged and appealed to by his own people, even by his parents, who protested that they would return to his sect even at the risk of losing their temporal goods if he would achieve victory over the Catholics by his arguments. But he no longer had any wish to continue the debate.' So said one side. The Donatists' version of the affair would have been entirely different. It is not hard to guess the thoughts of Emeritus. He had good reason to think 'the risk' of open opposition at that stage was not worth taking. There could well have been a horse for him too.

Chapter Twenty-Nine

THE CITY OF GOD

Two of the more than ninety books Augustine wrote have attained particular fame. Best known of all is his *Confessions.* Second must stand *The City of God*, five times as long, running to over a thousand pages. Not everyone finds the *Confessions* easy reading in spite of the personal story it tells, but *The City of God* is much more difficult, lacks a connecting thread of narrative and contains substantial passages of interest only to specialists. It is divided into five parts arranged in twenty-two books, each of which has a number of short chapters. Many have been repelled by its size and the large number of topics treated in what appears to be a chaotic tome, but for the determined reader it offers rich rewards. Augustine wrote it in his maturer years from 413 to 426, starting when he was fifty-nine and completing 'this huge work' when he was seventy-two.

Many of his other writings were composed to counter some doctrinal or practical threat to the faith, their Latin titles starting ominously with the word *Contra*, but *The City of God* was not written 'against' anybody, though it set out to challenge the contemporary inclination to blame Christianity for the fall of Rome. Scarcely mentioning Donatism or Pelagianism, it constitutes a marvellous revelation of Augustine's alert mind ranging over the Bible and many aspects of life around him. Read carefully and repeatedly, with omissions to suit each reader's taste, it proves to be not a dark tunnel but a colourful pageant in which we meet hundreds of citizens of Roman Africa and get to know its most famous man as we can nowhere else. The *Confessions* shows us Augustine lost in life's maze, until found at last. 'You have made us for Yourself,' he declared in its opening lines, 'and our hearts are restless till they rest in You.' That restlessness and that rest he captured brilliantly in the more popular book. But in *The City of God* he had passed a long way down life's road. The latest incident in the *Confessions* occurred when he was thirty-two. In *The City of God*, begun twenty-seven years later, he surveyed not himself but the world around him, the Christian Church in the world, and the message of the Bible to Church and world alike. In the *Confessions* we meet the convert; in *The City of God* we meet the bishop at his maximum height of intellectual, prophetic and expository genius. Thus the two books belong together : the second is the ultimate fruit of the first.

The title, *The City of God*, has dramatic biblical roots in the last chapters of the Epistle to the Hebrews and the Book of Revelation. It stands in contrast to Rome, the city of man, which had fallen at last. Throughout the book Augustine throws out memorable statements to show what he means by it. 'We, His City'; 'The City of God, that is to say, God's Church'; 'The pilgrim City of God, the redeemed household of servants of the Lord Christ'; 'Christians, the citizens of the Holy City of God, as they live by God's standards in the pilgrimage of this present life.' Apart from Rome, the counterpart to the City of God was another spiritual city, the devil's. 'I classify the human race into two branches : the one consists of those who live by human standards, the other of those who live according to God's will. I also call these two classes two cities, speaking allegorically. By two cities I mean two societies of human beings, one of which is predestined to reign with God for all eternity, the other doomed to undergo eternal punishment with the devil.' And he describes the City of God as itself consisting of two parts : the saints and angels already in heaven, and Christians still on pilgrimage in this world. So he repeatedly refers to 'the pilgrim City of God', declaring that 'the heavenly city leads what we may call a life of captivity in this earthly city, as in a foreign land,

and while on pilgrimage in this world she calls out citizens from all nations and so collects a society of aliens, speaking all languages.' This framework of ideas underlies the entire book. In expounding and illustrating it, apparently oblivious to time and length, Augustine's writing is rarely tedious and he so repeatedly captures our admiration by paragraphs of remarkable brilliance that, in spite of all its difficulties, *The City of God* retains its position among the great books of the world.

It also shows that the bishop of Hippo, toiling in his study, church and monastery, was by no means impervious to natural phenomena in the world around him. Amidst weightier matters it reveals his interest in very small creatures, in mice, newts, locusts, beetles, bees, flies, fleas, worms and frogs, for he frequently mentions them. He was aware that no kite 'however solitary as he hovers over his prey, does not find a mate, build a nest, help to hatch the eggs and rear the young birds'. Walking on the beach at Utica near Carthage one day he saw a huge molar which he supposed to be human, though he reckoned it was a hundred times the size of a normal tooth. And he was perplexed to know how wild animals came to be on the remoter Mediterranean islands. 'There are some islands situated so far from the mainland that it is clearly impossible for any beasts to have swum to them.' If men or angels did not take them there, he thought the earth itself must have produced them in these inaccessible places. On natural history in general he remarked that 'we see a constant succession as some things pass away and others arise, as the weaker succumb to the stronger and those that are overwhelmed adopt the qualities of their conquerors, and thus we have a pattern of a world of continual transcience'. He was aware that 'the variations of the seasons depend on the approach and withdrawal of the sun, and the waxing and waning of the moon produces growth and diminution in certain species, such as sea urchins and shellfish, and also the marvellous variations of the tides'.

He was convinced that there were 'immense tracts of space outside the world' and that the place occupied by the earth was 'so tiny a space compared with that infinity'. He suggested that the better an observer's sight the more stars he sees 'and so we are justified in supposing that some stars are invisible even to the keenest eyes quite apart from those which, we are assured, rise and set in another part of the world far removed from us'. Of that other part he seems only to have been vaguely aware of India, 'where men practise philosophy in nakedness and hence are called gymnosophists'. He thought Asia covered half the world, Europe and Africa the other half, and 'the reason why Europe and Africa are treated as two separate parts is that between them the water enters from the Ocean to form the intervening sea, our Great Sea'.

In *The City of God* Augustine expressed his regret that most people were so ignorant of history, for his own studies had led him to the conclusion that 'only illiterates imagine there is something extraordinary in the mishaps of their own time and that they did not happen in other periods'. The horrors of the past and the shocking realities of the present were part of his daily thinking. 'I am sick of recalling the many acts of revolting injustice, all the torrents of bloodshed, all the greed and monstrous cruelty, the disgusting infection of crime and immorality which rages, and the lust for power which of all human vices was found in its most concentrated form in the Roman people as a whole.' He lamented the pursuit of perverted delights by the freedom-loving majority whose spokesmen maintained that 'anyone should be free to do as he likes', arguing for a plentiful supply of prostitutes and proposing that 'anyone who disapproved of this kind of happiness should rank as a public enemy'. The cruelty of the courts, 'the wickedness of the wise man in his judicial capacity', deeply distressed him. He found it 'an unthinkable horror that innocent witnesses should be tortured in cases which are no concern of theirs, or that the accused are frequently overcome by the anguish of their pain and so make confessions and are punished despite their innocence, so that the judge still does not know whether it was a guilty or an innocent person he has executed'.

Surveying the social and moral conditions of the Empire, Augustine deduced that he was living in a world 'full of the allurements of impure pleasures, maddened with all its monstrous cruelties, menacing with all its errors and terrors'. When Rome's very triumphs had given way to 'wars of a worse kind, social and civil wars', he asked whether it was sensible to boast of the extent and grandeur of the Empire when 'you cannot show that men lived in happiness as they passed their lives under the shadow of fear and amid the terrors of ruthless ambition'. In addition to these public evils, he was constantly confronted with distressing personal situations, with men whose limbs never stopped shaking, others whose arms or legs had had to be amputated, some who were blind as well as deaf, one whose 'spine was so curved as to bring his hands to the ground, turning the man into a virtual quadruped', and many who had gone raving mad. 'Who is competent, however torrential the flow of his eloquence, to unfold all the miseries of this life?'

In spite of this catalogue of horrors, he did not agree with those who considered suicide justifiable to escape pain, torture or rape. To prevent rape by suicide was, in his opinion, merely adding one's own crime to the other person's. 'It is significant that in the sacred canonical books there can nowhere be found any injunction or permission to commit suicide, either to ensure immortality or to avoid evil. In fact we must understand it to be forbidden by the law "You shall not kill" (Exodus 20 : 13), particularly since there is no addition of "your neighbour" as in the prohibition of false witness. To kill oneself is to kill a human being and those guilty of their own death are not received after that death into a better life.'

It was also in *The City of God* that Augustine was able to divorce himself from the pressure of episcopal duties which normally dictated the course of his writing. Here he found time to contemplate 'the natural abilities of the human mind and the astounding achievements of human industry' in agriculture and navigation, in pottery and sculpture, in painting and poetry, in the capturing and taming of wild animals, in making weapons to destroy life and improving medical care to preserve it, in music, geometry, arithmetic and astronomy. 'It is God who has given man his mind,' he declared. He saw unmistakable evidence of the same 'Almighty Artist' in the versatile human body with its 'complex system of veins, sinews and internal organs', its erect posture so different from that of 'irrational animals which generally have their faces turned towards the ground', and the marvellous mobility of tongue and hand, 'so adapted for speaking and writing and for the accomplishment of a multitude of arts and crafts'.

To these good gifts of God he added 'the diversity of beauty in sky and earth and sea; the abundance of light and its miraculous loveliness in sun, moon and stars'; the charm of fire, so useful 'with its heat, its comfort and its help in cooking'; the multitudinous varieties of birds with their songs and their bright plumage; the countless different species of living creatures of all shapes and sizes; the abundant supply of food; the welcome alternation of day and night; the soothing coolness of breezes; all the material for clothing provided by plants and animals : and 'the mighty spectacle of the sea, putting on its changing colours like different garments, now green with many varied shades, now purple, now blue'.

In the final two hundred pages of the book Augustine set out his view of things to come. He had abandoned belief in a literal millennium and instead applied the term to the period 'from the first coming of Christ to the end of the world, which will be Christ's second coming'. Though he acknowledged that during this time the devil is allowed to test Christians, he was convinced that God had 'thrown him out from their inner man, the seat of belief in God, and tied him up among those who belong to his party'. From the con-

cluding verses of the Old Testament he deduced that Elijah
is to reappear and cause the Jews to turn to Christ. After that
he anticipated a brief period of intense persecution under
Antichrist, followed by Christ's return, the resurrection of
the dead, the last judgment and the splendour of the New
Jerusalem. He thought he was probably right in suggesting
this order of events, though he admitted there were many obscure statements in the Book of Revelation, 'principally because our author repeats the same thing in many ways, so that
he appears to be speaking of different matters though in fact
he is treating of the same subject in different terms'.

Augustine was emphatic that the punishment of unrepentant sinners will be eternal. He rejected the opinion of 'compassionate Christians' that God in His love would never allow
such a thing. 'Our friends who long to get rid of eternal
punishment should cease to argue against God and instead
obey God's commands while there is still time.' It was obvious
to him that 'the phrases "eternal punishment" and "eternal
life" are parallel' and that it was unwise for people to suppose
'that what is to happen is not what the Scriptures speak of
but what they themselves would like to happen'.

Then he surveyed the bliss in store for those who have been
emancipated from the powers of darkness and transferred
into the kingdom of Christ, 'liberated from this life of misery,
a kind of hell on earth, through the grace of Christ our
Saviour, our God and our Lord'. He looked forward to true
peace under no attack from within or without, when God
would be seen uninterruptedly, perfect freedom of the will
would be experienced together with the inability to sin, and
everything unlovely would be excluded. In gazing towards
this goal, however, Augustine was in no mood to encourage
complacency. He had stern words for those of disreputable
morals who thought they were safe because they were good
Catholics. 'What does the fact of baptism profit anyone if he
is not made righteous?' And in the middle of all his talk
about heaven he suddenly turned on himself along with his

readers. 'We must be on guard to make sure we are not deceived by clever talk into believing evil to be good or good evil, lest hostility provoke us into returning evil for evil, or immoderate sadness overwhelm us, or an unthankful heart make us sluggish in doing acts of kindness, or a clear conscience become wearied by malicious gossip, while our ill-founded suspicion of others leads us astray or others' false suspicion of us breaks our spirits. We must watch against the danger that sin makes us obey our bodies' cravings, that our eyes may be the servants of our desires, that longing for revenge may overcome us, that our imagination may dwell on wrongful delights, that we may listen with pleasure to indecent talk, that our liking and not God's law may govern our actions, that in this conflict we should expect to win the victory in our own strength instead of by the grace of Him who "gives us the victory through our Lord Jesus Christ" '. He was not prepared to offer heaven to anyone on easy terms.

Chapter Thirty

THE ERRING AND THE OBSTINATE

Augustine was usually working on more than one book at a time. Whatever he was treating as his main task, he was always ready to drop it and give priority to some new project when asked to do so. Long after beginning to write *The City of God* he completed his substantial volume on *The Trinity* which had occupied him at intervals for seventeen years. 'In my youth I began it,' he commented wistfully, 'and in my old age I have finished it.' At one point he ceased dictating when he discovered that several chapters had been 'filched from me before I deemed them worthy of publication under my name'. Eventually he recovered from this rude interference with his rigorous standards of revision and decided to finish the book.

One day in 420 a large crowd assembled on a square near the sea in Carthage, listening attentively to the public reading of a book whose theme was that the God of the Old Testament was a wicked demon and should be sharply distinguished from the God of the New Testament. Someone who was distressed by this sent a copy to Augustine, begging him to refute it without delay. At once he dropped other tasks to respond to this emergency.

He did so again to answer Vincentius Victor, a youth in Mauretania who had belonged to the Rogatists, the Donatist splinter group led by Augustine's old friend Vincentius. Although Victor had recently become a Catholic, he still retained such admiration for Vincentius that he had taken his name. He read a book by Augustine in which the bishop admitted that he was uncertain whether each person was given his soul separately by God at birth or received it through his parents along with his body, stating also that the soul was not body but spirit. To this Victor objected, so he wrote two books against Augustine's views. He let it be known that Vincentius had appeared to him in a vision and told him exactly how to go about this.

The bishop of Hippo frankly admired his young opponent's ability and eloquence. 'He possesses in no slight degree the faculty of explaining and beautifying what he thinks. All that is lacking is that he should first take care to think rightly.' He could not agree with Victor's assertion that 'we consist of spirit, soul and body, and all three are bodies', nor with his attempts to prove that the Bible teaches that souls are 'distinct acts of creation, breathed afresh into each individual'. With his usual extraordinary thoroughness Augustine dictated *The Soul and its Origin* in which he answered in some fifty thousand words the many errors into which he felt Victor was falling. 'You would undoubtedly be a wise man,' he told him, 'if only you did not believe that you were one already.' He himself refused to go beyond Scripture in making statements about the soul which he could not substantiate. 'I simply hold what I see the apostle has most plainly taught us, that owing to one man all who are born of Adam pass into condemnation unless they are born again in Christ—even as He, the most merciful bestower of grace, appointed those whom he predestined to everlasting life to be regenerated. To those whom He predestined to eternal death He is also the righteous awarder of punishment, not only on account of the sins which they add in the indulgence of their own will, but also because of their original sin, even if, as in the case of infants, they add nothing to it.'

Not all the emergencies concerned matters of belief. After the suppression of the Donatists there came to be many new Catholics in the country town of Fussala, forty miles from Hippo. Partly because of the distance but primarily because the people there were not well acquainted with the Latin language, Augustine found it difficult to give them proper care. He succeeded in finding an apparently suitable Punic-speaking man whom he proposed to appoint bishop of Fussala, so he persuaded the elderly primate of Numidia to make a long journey and officiate at the ordination. To his dismay the candidate withdrew at the last moment. In this predicament Augustine put forward a youth named Antonius, who had been with him from childhood in the monastery, and on his recommendation both the primate and the people of Fussala accepted him.

Howevere, he was not a success. While Augustine regarded accusations of immorality made against him as groundless, there could be no doubt that the local congregation had every reason to resent his tyrannical ways. He was misusing his office to enrich himself at their expense. Augustine felt compelled to interfere : he allowed Antonius to continue as bishop, but barred him from communion until he had made full financial restitution to his flock. To a certain extent Antonius submitted to this judgment, but he remained covetous, lording it over others. In this ongoing dispute Augustine tried, rather unsuccessfully, to support both sides. He was committed to dealing gently with the young man, 'my son in Christ', and also to retaining the confidence of the local population, since 'these unhappy men, being now Catholic Christians, dread greater evils from a Catholic bishop than those which, when they were heretics, they dreaded from the laws of Catholic emperors'. The people were so frustrated that they wrote to Augustine's friend, Caelestine, who had become bishop of Rome, complaining of his misjudgment in sending Antonius to them. This forced Augustine to explain the whole matter to Caelestine, admitting at the same time that 'I am so racked with anxiety and grief that I think of retiring from the responsibilities of the episcopal office.'

And not long afterwards he was in trouble over another young man, bishop Auxilius of Nurco, because of his high-handed treatment of an important official named Classicianus. A group of men who had fallen foul of the official

sought sanctuary in the church : ' Nurco. Classicianus came
with an escort and asked the bishop not to extend any privi-
leges to them. Later, the group judged it safe to leave of their
own accord and thus the incident could have been considered
closed. Auxilius, however, who had been bishop for less than
a year, took offence and decided to excommunicate the official along with all his family. Classicianus appealed to Augustine, who was inclined to accept his version of events and was
concerned lest some member of his household 'should perish
through departing from the body without baptism'. He
reasoned the matter out with Auxilius, for he saw no reason
why Classicianus himself should be punished in this way and
regarded it as preposterous that his family and servants were
included in the ban. 'I have never ventured to do as you have
done, for if anyone were to challenge me to justify such an
act I could give no satisfactory reply. But if the Lord has
revealed to you that it may be justly done, I by no means
despise your inexperience and I am ready to learn from one
who is but young if he undertakes to teach me how we can
justify our conduct if we inflict a spiritual punishment on
innocent souls because of another person's crime. Think not
that because we are bishops it is impossible for unjust resentment to gain secretly upon us. Let us rather remember that,
because we are men, our life in the midst of temptation's
snares is beset with the greatest possible dangers. Cancel,
therefore, the ecclesiastical sentence which, perhaps under
the influence of unusual excitement, you have passed. Let
strife be banished and peace invited to return, lest this man
who is your friend be lost to you and the devil who is your
enemy rejoice over you both.'

Resentment, temptation and excitement came still closer
home to Augustine around the year 420 when the last known
episode in the long struggle to liquidate the Donatist Church
took place. A dramatic situation developed which threatened
to match the mass suicide of the Jewish defenders of Massada
in the first century. An official named Dulcitius was sent from

Italy to strike the final blow by demanding the submission of the Donatists in south Numidia in much the same way as Macarius had done some seventy-five years before. On his arrival Dulcitius took the opportunity of sounding Augustine out on some biblical conundrums which were perplexing him, such as whether the witch of Endor really did call up the prophet Samuel, whether the last judgment will take place as soon as the Lord returns or not, and why God called so grave a sinner as David 'a man after my own heart'. Then he turned to the grim business of his visit and led his soldiers into those regions Augustine never sighted in all his life, the heart of Numidia where the Aures Mountains towered above Donatist farms and villages. He made for Timgad, where in earlier days bishop Optatus had sided with Gildo against the Romans. For in Timgad, even nine years after the Carthage Conference, the great Donatist cathedral still maintained its independence with Gaudentius, one of the spokesmen on that occasion, now its defiant bishop.

'We should pray that all who carry the standard of Christ against Christ', Augustine wrote to Dulcitius, 'and boast of the gospel against the gospel, may forsake their wrong way and rejoice with us in the unity of Christ.' But the men of Timgad, eyeing the well-armed imperial forces closing in on them, saw no gospel, no Christ, and no love, but only devilishness and oppression. From the threats Dulcitius uttered they perceived that exile and death were to be their lot. So Gaudentius and his people determined, like the defenders of Massada, that they would deny the Romans the chance of deciding their fate. The great church compound, covering some five acres, was turned into a fortress packed with Donatist Christians, and Gaudentius informed Dulcitius that they would burn it down over their own heads if they were attacked.

The confrontation lasted several months. There was time for Gaudentius to write to Dulcitius, for the tribune to send the letters back to Augustine in Hippo, and for the latter to compose a considerable answer, grimly entitled *Against Gaudentius*. The Donatist leader reminded the officer he was facing, and the bishop who was the driving force behind him, that 'the Saviour of souls, the Lord Christ, sent fishermen, not soldiers, to make the faith known'. He denied that God, the judge of the living and the dead, looked for the help of a worldly army. He suggested they might like to remember the words of Christ Himself about the good shepherd who laid down His life for the sheep and the wolf who 'attacks the flock and scatters it' (John 10 : 12). He could see no 'safe and peaceful harbour' for himself and other leaders 'tossed from every quarter in this stormy persecution' because 'those who might give refuge to Christians, terrified by the proscriptions and fearful of danger, not only do not receive them but are even afraid to meet those whom they venerate in silence.' He felt the Donatists were in a worse position than the original apostles whom the Lord told to flee from one town to another, because in those days people who sheltered them were not liable to severe punishment.

Augustine saw it all quite differently. 'They cannot have the death of martyrs,' he declared, 'because they do not have the life of Christians.' He had met this threat to commit suicide before, 'the mad aberration of a few men', and he was not going to be moved by it. 'It is better for some of them to perish in their own fire,' he said, 'than that all should equally burn in the eternal fires of hell as a punishment for their accursed dissension.'

History was not so kind to Gaudentius and his men as to the defenders of Massada. No grateful descendants commemorate their stand, and it is not known what happened to them. The massive triumphal archway, standing guard over the paved roads and ruined houses of Timgad to this day, tells no tales.

PART SIX

420–430

THE HUMBLING YEARS

Chapter Thirty-One

THE VOICE OF JULIAN

By the time Gaudentius had taken his stand as the last known champion of Donatism, Augustine had been compelled to turn his attention to a new opponent. A certain bishop Memor had frequently written to him from Italy, pleading for copies of his books. Through correspondence 'he was joined with me in no slight friendship'. So when Possidius had occasion to visit Italy, Augustine took the opportunity of sending Memor a parcel of books and a letter which ended with the words, 'May the shadow of the wings of the Most High be for ever the dwelling place of you all who with oneness of heart occupy one home, father and mother bound in the same brotherhood with your sons, being all the children of one Father.' Amongst these sons was a boy named Julian, whom Augustine hoped might come over and join him in Hippo.

'As a deacon he is engaged in the same warfare as ourselves,' he told Memor, 'and while I dare not say that I love him more than I love you, yet this I may say that I long for him more than I long for you.' But they were never to meet. In 417 Julian became bishop of Eclanum in the mountains behind Naples. By that time he was thirty-two, married to the daughter of another bishop, and fast becoming the new spokesman of Pelagianism, not at all impressed by his father's old friend. The Catholic Church in Italy soon decided to take disciplinary action against him. In 419 he was deposed and exiled in accordance with edicts issued by Honorius against any bishop who did not prove his orthodoxy by condemning the views of Pelagius. He went first to Cilicia and spent the rest of his life as a critic on the run. He dispatched a letter to the bishop of Rome openly attacking Augustine's views and joined seventeen others in sending a similar one to the bishop of Thessalonica. When Alypius was staying briefly with the bishop of Rome in 420 he was given copies of both these letters to take back to Augustine, who lost no time in dictating elaborate treatises defending himself and answering Julian in great detail. Thus battle was joined between them.

No quarter was given. To Julian, Augustine was 'the Carthaginian', a kind of modern Hannibal threatening the Romans, the enemy of both marriage and free will, the distorter of the character of God, the advocate of fatalism, still profoundly influenced by the Manicheism he claimed to have abandoned. To Augustine, Julian was a mad perverter of Christian truth, an enemy of the grace of God and a poisoner of the minds of men, 'tearing in pieces the sheep redeemed at such a price'. When Julian tried to re-establish himself in Italy he was again expelled. Finding refuge in Constantinople, he was eventually driven from there too. Repeatedly rejected and condemned by Church councils, he paid a high price for his obstinacy and has been pilloried for heresy along with Pelagius through succeeding ages.

As usual with opponents of the bishop of Hippo, we know Julian's views mainly thanks to quotations Augustine made from his writings in order to refute them. The issues on which they differed were the doctrine of original sin and the precise relationship between God's grace and human free will, but these involved disagreement on such related matters as marriage, the sexual instinct, the fate of infants dying unbaptised and the efficacy of baptism. Augustine accused Julian of five major errors. He blamed him for 'Praise of the Creature', since he alleged that men were so much the work of God that sin was not a defect in their nature but a misuse of their free will. He blamed him for 'Praise of Marriage', since he taught that infants were born sinless. He blamed him for 'Praise of the Law', since he identified the Mosaic law with grace by saying that those who kept it were given eternal life. He

blamed him for 'Praise of Free Will', because his statement
that 'grace assists the good purpose of everyone' implied that
the good purpose came first and was then rewarded by God's
grace. He blamed him for 'Praise of Saints', for he believed
that after baptism men were without sin. In addition he
accused Julian of calling the will of Almighty God by the
name of fate, of depriving infants of the aid of Christ, of
teaching that as a creature made by God the human soul is
upright and of making out that sexual desire is natural and
good.

On his part Julian was just as dogmatic in denouncing
Augustine for treating sexual desire, including the intercourse of married people, as an evil thing, thus denigrating
the whole marriage relationship. 'Married people are not
guilty,' he insisted. 'The sexual impulse is ordained by God.
Your assertion amounts to saying that original sin is actually
derived from marriage.' He accused Augustine of denying
any real free will to mankind and strongly protested against
his view that God has predestined some to salvation, others
to damnation. 'No one is forced by God's power either into
evil or into good,' he declared. 'Man does good or evil of his
own free will, assisted by God's grace or incited by the sug-
gestions of the devil.'

These formidable charges and countercharges proved to
be merely the preliminary skirmishes of a prolonged verbal
war. Augustine sternly warned his young antagonist that 'if,
by the help of her sons who possess authority in the state,
your Catholic mother acts with a view to making you afraid,
she does so not from cruelty but out of love'. Undeterred by
such threats, Julian lost no time in publishing a lengthy re-
joinder. Weighing up the bishop's views he described him as
'an insect which is a nuisance when alive and emits a foul
stench after it has been crushed'. He declared Augustine's
theology to be totally deformed, since it ascribed to God the
grossest injustice in His treatment of infants and of the
damned. Detecting clear traces of dualism in the role Augus-

tine attributed to the devil in the shaping of man's nature, he announced that the bishop of Hippo and his friends were a gang of Manichean bandits bent on abducting the Christian Church.

Confronted with such hard-hitting language, Augustine defended himself with equal vigour, telling Julian to 'shut your impudent mouth'. Julian did nothing of the sort. 'If God created men,' he shouted back, 'they cannot be born with any evil in them; if marriage is good, nothing evil arises from it; if all sins are forgiven in baptism, the children of the born again cannot contract original sin; if God is just, He cannot condemn children for the sins of their parents; if human nature is capable of righteousness, it cannot have natural faults.' He insisted it was ridiculous to regard new-born infants as offenders. To Augustine's view that predestination by God has nothing whatever to do with human merit he retorted that 'what is not the result of merit is the result of fate'.

Point by point Augustine resisted him through hundreds of pages in his *Against Julian,* written in 421. Of course he knew a lot more about Manicheism than Julian did, and he could set out an array of Scripture texts in support of his views, reinforcing his interpretation of them by the arguments of other learned divines, above all by quotations from Ambrose 'whom I revere as a father, for in Christ Jesus he begat me through the gospel'. Over and over again he analysed the story of Adam and Eve. Over and over again he delved into the mysteries of marriage, sexual instinct and the procreation of children. And somehow he still professed his affection for Julian, 'which by God's mercy you shall not remove from the fibres of my heart by any insults'.

There the matter rested for the time being. Each man felt that his case was unanswerable. 'You are mistaken, my son,' announced Augustine in conclusion, 'wretchedly mistaken'.

Chapter Thirty-Two
THE BIBLE NEVER LIES

Throughout his Christian life Augustine remained an enthusiastic champion of the Bible. To him it was unique, the
one indispensable book, in which the Spirit of God speaks
through human authors. 'The Bible never lies.' It was his
intention that everything he preached or wrote should be
'either what I found stated in Scripture or what I could infer
from scriptural statements, always keeping in conformity
with the authority of the Bible'. He recognised no higher
authority. 'For our part we abide by the language of Scripture, which is the basis of our Christian belief.' Convinced
that it was inspired by God, he kept up such intensive study
of the Bible that, like Jerome, he was able to quote from all
parts of it with extraordinary facility, though unaided by the
chapter and verse divisions of later times.

This did not imply, however, that he was blind to the value
of the great non-Christian writers of antiquity, to some of
whom he had been so deeply indebted. He retained an affection for Cicero and never lost his respect for Plato. In *The
City of God* he reviewed the works of many famous authors,
including Aristotle, 'a man of commanding genius, no match
for Plato in literary style but still far above the general run',
but he set a wide chasm between the greatest productions of
human genius and the Bible. 'The prophets were taught by
God's Spirit, whereas the philosophers were misled by
human speculation. Platonist philosophers excel all others
just because they are nearer to the truth than the rest, even
though they are a long way from it.'

Augustine regarded the Old Testament Apocrypha as a
genuine part of the Bible. He frequently quoted 'The Wisdom

of Solomon' and 'Ecclesiasticus', referring more sparingly to 'Tobit' and other books. Although he denied Solomon's authorship of anything in the Apocrypha, he felt that the Church had from earliest times accepted these books, while not giving so much weight to them as to those included in the Jewish canon. Later writings disseminated in the name of Enoch and other prophets he did not accept, nor 'more recent productions under the names of apostles', because of their obscure origin and the manifest falsehoods they contained.

The number of different Bibles current in his day caused him some problems. In addition to the Hebrew and Greek originals, he had to cope with the Septuagint translation of the Old Testament into Greek, the Latin Bible he himself used — nowadays known as the Old Latin — and Jerome's new version. There was, for example, considerable discrepancy between the ages of the patriarchs recorded in the Hebrew and the Old Latin, giving rise to 'that notorius problem that Methusalah, by our reckoning, lived for fourteen years after the flood', which he attributed to a scribal error. Differences between the Hebrew and the Septuagint were perplexing to him because of the tradition of the miraculous origin of the latter and the numerous quotations from it in the New Testament. To solve this dilemma Augustine fell back on the idea that the seventy translators were just as much prophets as the original authors. 'We are justified in supposing that they received the spirit of prophecy and so, if they altered anything and used expressions in their translation different from those of the original, we should not doubt that these expressions were also inspired by God.'

We have already seen that Augustine was inclined to resist the innovation of Jerome's work. 'Our time has produced the presbyter Jerome, a man of great learning and a master of all three languages. He has translated the Scriptures into Latin, not from the Greek but from the Hebrew. The Jews acknowledge the reliability of the fruit of his learned labours and maintain that the seventy translators were mistaken in many places. Nevertheless it is the judgment of the churches of Christ that no one man should be preferred to the authority of so large a body of men.' History, however, was to overturn his verdict : the Vulgate triumphed; the Old Latin became obsolete.

In interpreting Scripture Augustine emphasised the historical sense but was prone to search for symbolic meanings as well. In his view all the elaborate details in the story of Noah's ark were designed to present a prophetic picture of the Christian Church, though he did his best to maintain a balanced attitude. 'In my opinion it is a complete mistake to suppose that no narrative of events in this type of literature has any significance beyond the purely historical record, but it is equally rash to hold that every single statement in these books is a complex of allegorical meanings. In spite of that, I do not censure those who have succeeded in carving out a spiritual meaning from each and every event in the narrative, provided they have maintained its original basis of historical truth.' However, this did not save him from saying that Noah's drunkenness was a symbol of Christ's passion. 'He was drunk, that is, he suffered.' He considered that the wine Noah drank prefigured the cup at the Last Supper, his nakedness the Saviour's crucifixion, and the wood of which the ark was made pointed to the cross 'on which was suspended the Mediator'. Even extravagances of this kind testify to his sense of the relevance of every line of Scripture.

Augustine's special talent was not so much for expounding hidden meanings in the Old Testament as for presenting the truths of the New Testament. 'Obedience,' he used to say, 'is the mother and guardian of all the other virtues', and he was equally certain that 'there is an evil spirit which drives men's minds to wickedness by a secret compulsion, goading them on to commit adultery'. Tirelessly he proclaimed the message of the gospel. 'Peace between mortal man and God is an ordered obedience, in faith, in subjection to an everlasting law. When we were overwhelmed by the load of our sins He sent to us His Word, His only Son, who was born and who suffered in the flesh He assumed for our sake, so that we might come to know the value God placed on mankind and might be purified from all sins by that unique sacrifice so that, when love had been diffused in our hearts by His Spirit and when all difficulties had been surmounted, we might come to eternal rest.'

To the end of his life he continued to wrestle with the Bible, freely admitting that 'even our probing of the Scriptures is laborious'. When he could not understand it, he was not ashamed to say so. 'I confess that the meaning of this completely escapes me' was his comment on 2 Thessalonians 2 :6–7. When he was sure of its message he did not mince his words. 'There is one road, and only one, secured against all possibility of going astray, provided by One who is both God and man. As God He is the goal. As man He is the way. Apart from this way no one has been set free, no one is being set free, no one will be set free. This is the right road, which leads to the vision of God and to eternal union with Him. It is asserted and proclaimed in the truth of the Holy Scriptures.'

Chapter Thirty-Three

MONKS AND MIRACLES

Ever since the end of the fourth century the number of monks had been increasing in Africa. Most of them had previously been slaves, peasants or craftsmen, although some former landowners and businessmen were to be found in the monasteries. Augustine was convinced that monks ought to support themselves by manual labour, basing his opinion primarily on Paul's advice in 2 Thessalonians 3 :6–13, which includes the words, 'If any one will not work, let him not eat.' However, not all agreed with this and Aurelius asked his help in dealing with some monks at Carthage who were quoting Christ against Paul, particularly His sayings in the Sermon on the Mount referring to birds and lilies and not being anxious about food or clothing.

Augustine felt that these men, who expected to be supported by the gifts of working people, were simply giving way to laziness. He was concerned to find that their admirers 'preached them up as holier men'. In his view responsible monasticism, which combined study and prayer with regular hours set apart for 'a common workman's lowly toil', was being brought into disrepute by 'so many hypocrites under the garb of monks, strolling about the provinces, sent nowhere, fixed nowhere, standing nowhere, sitting nowhere, some hawking about the limbs of martyrs—if indeed of martyrs—', and all of them asking for money. He did not hesitate to call such behaviour devilish. And he also denounced the habit some of them had of letting their hair grow long. 'I shrink from saying more against this fault out of respect for certain long-haired brethren in whom, except for this, I find much to admire.'

There were always other clergy living with Augustine, sharing his meals, clothed from a common fund and subject to the discipline he imposed. Although they used silver spoons, food was served in humbler dishes of clay, wood or marble and there was not a great deal of it. Guests and those who were unwell might get meat. Soup and vegetables were occasionally included. 'There was wine at all times,' a fixed allowance liable to be cut if anyone broke the rule prohibiting swearing. The chief interest at meal times was not the food but reading and conversation, though Augustine found it necessary to put up a notice saying 'He who would injure the name of an absent friend may not at this table as guest attend' and on one occasion threatened to leave the room when it was ignored.

In view of the size of his congregation he restricted his visiting to three categories of people : widows, orphans and the sick who called for him. To the latter he went without delay, laying his hands on them and praying over them. He visited the nearby nunnery only when it was absolutely necessary. His sister, whom he never named, had long presided there. When she died she was succeeded as prioress by Felicitas, who had been her assistant, while a new man named Rusticus became prior at the nunnery. However, the arrangement did not work well. The nuns wanted to get rid of Felicitas and some people thought this was due to the influence of Rusticus.

Augustine himself had devised the rule under which the nuns lived. All property, including their clothes, was held in common. Girls from poor homes found themselves living in comparative luxury, while others had to learn a new discipline. Any presents brought by parents for their daughters were not kept for private use, but added to the common stock under control of the prioress. To conceal a gift received was treated as theft. There were regular times of prayer and of fasting, but a bath was allowed only once a month. Meals were taken in silence, listening to a reader. Hair had to be completely covered. No one was allowed to look fixedly at any man, particularly in church. 'A wanton eye is the index of a wanton heart.' The nuns were expected to warn one another should 'wanton hearts exchange signals with each other'. Persistent offenders were to be reported, brought before the prioress and eventually before the whole sisterhood, with expulsion as the ultimate punishment. The prioress was to be obeyed as a mother charged with the special responsibility of seeing that the rules were observed. Negative though most of these regulations may seem, it has to be remembered that Augustine was providing an alternative way of life for girls in a harsh world where they were often married off, uneducated, at twelve years of age and many must have entered the nunnery at that stage in their lives. So he was anxious to support Felicitas. 'Under her you spent your noviciate, under her you took the veil, under her your number has been multiplied, and yet you are riotously demanding that she should be replaced by another.'

When Orosius had returned to Africa from Palestine, he brought with him some bits of bone and handfuls of dust which were alleged to be relics of the early Christian martyr, Stephen. Someone had had a vision as a result of which these scraps were unearthed at Gaza. An irrational veneration of martyrs and their supposed remains had become very popular in the century since state persecution of Christians had ceased, but for several years Augustine did not actively promote the cult. These bogus relics of Stephen, killed in Jerusalem almost four hundred years previously, were deposited in small shrines throughout Roman Africa. Evodius had a little vessel supposed to contain some of his blood. There came to be a shrine of St. Stephen at Calama and another on an estate called Andurus. Then in 424 Augustine's colleague Eraclius built a chapel containing a few grains of the venerated dust alongside the church at Hippo.

Augustine did not oppose the innovation. In fact he was increasingly impressed by the miracles of healing which were reported to have occurred in connection with the relics. In one of his sermons he declared that 'Stephen has visited our country after his death'. In an age when there was little relief for pain, stories of alleged cures had tremendous appeal. Augustine remembered that Ambrose had been shown in a vision where two martys were buried; when their bodies were exhumed and taken into the church in Milan blind people regained their sight and those tormented by evil spirits were healed. There was a natural tendency to welcome and exaggerate miraculous events which seemed to confirm faith. Feeling that 'signs of divine power like those of olden days were frequently occurring in modern times too', Augustine initiated public readings of such stories so that they might be 'pounded into the memory as gravel is pounded into a path'.

He knew a bishop, waiting for an operation on a painful ulcer, who was instantly healed while carrying relics of Stephen in a procession. A blind woman was cured by pressing to her eyes a bunch of flowers carried by another bishop while he held the relics. A priest died at Calama, 'his thumbs were already tied together', but when someone rushed his tunic to the martyr's shrine and then laid it on his body, he recovered. A child playing in the square at Andurus was crushed by the wheel of a runaway ox cart and lay writhing at the point of death. 'His mother snatched him up and placed him in the shrine. He not only revived but showed no sign of injury.' One marvel begat another. Raisings from the dead followed thick and fast, thanks either to clothes taken to shrines and hurried back to the body, or to prayer as the corpse lay beside the relics, or to anointing with St. Stephen's oil. Each healing was instantaneous and perfect, growing more fantastic at every telling. Truth and lies became inextricably intertwined.

A climax was reached with the coming of the Cappadocian tremblers. The story was that seven brothers and three sisters in Cappadocia had been laid under such a curse by their widowed mother that they were all afflicted with a dreadful trembling. The sight proved so fascinating to their fellow citizens that all ten of them 'took to wandering wherever the whim suggested and in this way visited almost every part of the Roman world'. When two of these professional beggars, Paulus and his sister Palladia, visited Africa they created a great sensation. 'They arrived at Hippo about a fortnight before Easter and attended church every day, visiting the shrine of the glorious martyr Stephen.'

On Easter Sunday morning, when a huge congregation had assembled, Paulus was the centre of attraction, holding on to the grating of the shrine as he prayed. Suddenly he fell flat on his face and then stood up, healed. 'The whole church was filled in every corner with shouts of thanksgiving,' Augustine recorded. 'They ran with the news to me where I was sitting, ready for the procession. They came rushing one after another, each telling me, as though it was fresh news, what I had been told by the one before.' Paulus too presented himself to the bishop, 'bent down at my knees, then straightened himself up to receive my kiss'. They went into the church, packed to the doors with an excited mass of people, shouting with joy and praising God. 'At last silence was restored and the appointed lessons from Holy Scripture were read.'

After Augustine had preached, 'the man had breakfast with us and gave a detailed account of the whole tragic history of himself, his brothers, his sisters, and his mother'. Augustine had an official record of the event drawn up and on the following Wednesday there was another great gathering. 'I made the brother and sister stand on the steps of the bishop's throne, just below the level from which I addressed the people, while the narrative was read. The whole congregation, men and women alike, fixed their gaze on the pair, the brother standing without any untoward movement, the sister trembling in every limb.' He then asked the couple to withdraw while their case was discussed, but this was soon interrupted by loud shouts from the shrine containing the relics. No sooner had Palladia touched the grating than 'she fell down as if asleep and got up cured'. Pandemonium broke out when they brought her back into the church.

'Christian miracles,' declared Augustine, 'are the work of God with the cooperation of the martyrs.' Although he made no attempt to justify this assertion from the Bible, it became his conviction that because the martyrs of former times had suffered for speaking the truth 'they have the power to perform miracles'. So he encouraged a cult of relics which was destined to proliferate in succeeding centuries. Even in the deserted church on Cathedral Hill above the ruins of Hippo, where his effigy lies to this day, a piece of glass over the right forearm reveals what is supposed to be one of his own bones.

Chapter Thirty-Four

BONIFACE AND THE ARIANS

On August 15th, 423 the Emperor Honorius died childless after a twenty-eight year reign which had witnessed a long series of disasters for the Roman Empire. The husband of his half-sister Placidia had recently become co-emperor with him but died a few months later. A civil servant named John held sway for two years before Placidia's son Valentinian III, a child of six, was assured of the succession. So once again power was in a woman's hand.

Placidia had two relatively competent generals, Aetius in Italy and Count Boniface in Africa. There was no love lost between them, but Aetius was close to her and Boniface far away. Augustine had little chance to communicate with the Count and when at last he came to Hippo the bishop was ill and scarcely able to speak. At this juncture Boniface's wife died. Not long afterwards Augustine and Alypius met him at a place called Tubunae. To some extent the fate of Africa hinged upon their conference. Boniface felt ready to abandon public life and enter a monastery, but for once the two friends argued against it. They insisted he could render greater service to the Church if he protected Africa from the hordes of barbarians who were threatening the Empire. To their great relief at the time, he accepted their advice but soon afterwards they heard with regret that he had re-married. His new wife was an Arian Christian but Boniface required her to become a Catholic. Their daughter, however, was baptised by the Arians and tales of the Count's immoralities combined with this to make Augustine uneasy about him.

There were plenty of other things to keep Augustine busy.

He had embarked upon one of his more remarkable ventures in authorship. 'With a kind of judicial severity I am reviewing all my works and as it were with the pen of a censor, indicating what dissatisfies me.' The result was his *Retractations*, in which he also recorded the circumstances that had given rise to each book. One of the matters he clarified was his ambivalent interpretation of Christ's statement 'On this rock I will build my church' (Matthew 16 : 18). He admitted that in his earlier writings he had sometimes said that Peter himself was the rock, but later he had always taught that the Church was built on the faith Peter had just confessed in saying 'You are the Christ, the Son of the living God' (Matthew 16 : 16). He liked to connect this with Paul's words 'that rock was Christ' (1 Corinthians 10 : 4) and at times he expressly repudiated his previous view of the matter. 'Christ said to Peter, "I will build you upon Myself, not Myself upon you." Men who wished to be built upon men said, "I follow Paul and I Apollos and I Cephas" (who is Peter), but others, who did not wish to be built upon Peter but upon the Rock, said "I follow Christ" (1 Corinthians 1 : 12).' In the *Retractations* he did not correct these statements but reiterated them memorably. 'The Church is built on Him whom Peter confessed, for what Christ said to him was "You are Peter" (Matthew 16 : 18) not "You are Rock". The Rock was Christ.'

However busy he was dictating to his secretaries, he never forgot his calling as a pastor. 'I have torn myself away from many duties, or rather I have slipped away, stolen myself away from them to write to you, my oldest friend,' he told a man of his own age only recently turning towards the Church, urging him to enrol for baptism. To another in his late seventies, formerly with him in Manicheism, recently widowed and reported to be living with several concubines, he wrote, 'I am now an old man and a bishop as well, and you have not yet amended your life. I cannot forget your great services to me, but I am tortured by your conduct.

Hearken to God. Think of Christ. Listen to the Apostle. Why do you keep on sinning by putting off your conversion from day to day?'

He counselled the young as well. He wrote firmly to a wealthy girl with a small son who had persuaded her husband that they should go on living together but no longer sleep together. One day when she was alone at home two strangers called, wandering monks hoping for financial help. In her religious ardour she gave them clothing, money, silver, gold, in fact almost everything she had. They went off delighted, praising her charity, but when her husband returned and discovered what had happened he was furious. He cursed his wife and the monks — robbers so far as he was concerned — and in his despair went off with another woman. Augustine did not approve of that, yet he sympathised with the man's feelings. He told the girl that she had no right to give away their property without consulting her husband. 'I am grieved at his conduct, which is the result of your reckless and inconsiderate behaviour. Write him your apology, begging his pardon. Promise that in future you will be subject to him in everything. And as for your son, his father cannot be denied custody of him. Your union of hearts is necessary for him, so that he may be reared and trained in the wisdom of God.'

Then the storm of Count Boniface's life increased to a hurricane. It seems that Aetius persuaded Placidia to recall him and at the same time induced him to disobey her summons. During 427–8 two expeditions were mounted against him from Rome, and in the confusion of these events Gothic mercenaries arrived in Africa. The Goths were Arian Christians and along with them came some of their clergy. An Arian bishop named Maximinus settled for a time at Hippo. A rival bishop in the town was not something Augustine was prepared to overlook. He had originally encountered Arianism before his conversion in Milan. Its distinctive feature was that Arians maintained Christ was a created being, inferior to God the Father. They stressed such sayings of His as 'The Father is greater than I' (1 John 14 :28). To them the very title 'Son of God' implied inferiority and indicated that there was a time before He was begotten by the Father. There had never been many Arians in Africa, so when one of them wrote to Augustine in an attempt to convert him to their viewpoint, he replied with his tongue in his cheek, 'I am very grateful to you for trying to reclaim me from error, because you think I am wrong. May God reward your kindness in this and grant you to know what you think you know.'

On another occasion he approached an Arian doctor who had become a Catholic but did nothing to influence the rest of his family, telling him he should be ashamed to come to the house of God without those who lived in his own house. The years he had spent working on his book about the Trinity had made him most familiar with the points at issue, so he explained them to the doctor with his usual lucidity. 'The only begotten Son does not come from God the Father in the same way as the whole creation, which He created out of nothing. He begat the Son from his own substance. He did not make Him out of nothing. He did not beget Him in time, for as the flame is not antecedent to the brightness it produces so the Father has never been without the Son. Christ's reason for saying that the Father is greater is that He "emptied Himself, taking the form of a servant" (Philippians 2 :7) without losing that of God. Because of that form of God which He did not lose He said, "I and the Father are one." (John 10 :30). Therefore it is perfectly reasonable to say that Christ as man is less than the Father and that Christ as God is equal to the Father, is equally God.'

There had also been an encounter with Pascentius, a powerful Arian tax collector in Carthage, who enjoyed using his authority to pester Catholics. He had a very poor opinion of Augustine, comparing him to 'a thirsty man, parched with great heat, who finds muddy water and wallows in it'. They once met in public debate, Augustine having reluctantly agreed to Pascentius' terms that no record of proceedings should be taken down. An exchange of letters followed, though Augustine regarded the man as so dangerous that he was very careful what he committed to paper. Knowing this, Pascentius rather enjoyed taunting him in his replies. 'Finally, I say it with all due respect,' he wrote, 'the pattern of your belief is like a bent and knotted tree with nothing straight about it, an offence to the eye. You wrote to me that the Father is God, the Son is God, and the Holy Spirit is God —one God. How can there be one God from three?'

So when Maximinus appeared in Hippo, Augustine prepared for action. Another public debate was arranged and he insisted secretaries be present. As a newcomer Maximinus was a bold man to tackle Augustine on his home ground, but he proved a worthy opponent, so intellectually alert and biblically forearmed that it was a contest of giants. To the Catholics, Augustine routed his man. To Maximinus and his friends it was an equally resounding triumph over the Goliath of Catholicism and he cheerfully spread the word of his victory when he got back to Carthage. So, in addition to publishing his recapitulation of their dialogue, Augustine set to work on another exhaustive volume, *Against Maximinus*. At this stage in his life, assured of an extensive readership and with no shortage of secretarial help, he had become a compulsive writer. Possidius remembered that 'this treatise, being of the greatest length, occupied the whole span of days that remained to him.'

Chapter Thirty-Five

GRACE AND PREDESTINATION

Early in 426, when Augustine was seventy-two, two young men from a monastery at Hadrumetum, on the east coast of what is now Tunisia, arrived in Hippo. They told him that his books against Pelagius and Julian had occasioned grave differences of opinion in their brotherhood, some monks championing the grace of God and others human free will. As they wanted to get back for Easter, he hastily wrote a letter for them to take, but in the end detained them much longer and composed a treatise on *Grace and Free Will* specially for their company, reading it over with them along with other books to make sure they understood his point of view thoroughly.

That summer he travelled to the west of Numidia to visit the Church at Milevis. Their bishop had recently died and, although he had designated his successor to the local clergy, bitterness and strife resulted because his choice had never been made public. To avoid similar misunderstandings arising at Hippo, Augustine decided to convene a great assembly at which he announced amidst general enthusiasm that he wished Eraclius to succeed him. He devolved many of his duties to the younger man at once, promising to be available for consultation at any time.

Meanwhile the monks at Hadrumetum had been studying *Grace and Free Will*, in which Augustine asserted that 'God has revealed to us through His Holy Scriptures that there is in man a free choice of will', since this was presupposed by many commands which he quoted from both Testaments. However, most of the treatise was devoted to establishing the absolute necessity for the grace of God 'by which the human will is not taken away but changed from bad to good and assisted when good'. He argued that grace precedes faith, that Christians choose God because they have been chosen by Him, not vice versa, and that God does whatever He wills to do, 'to bestow kindness on some and to heap punishment on others, as He Himself judges right by a counsel secret to Himself but beyond all doubt most righteous'. So he made it quite clear which side in the dispute had his support. 'It is not so much I myself as the inspired Scripture which has spoken to you.'

However, the disagreement among the monks continued. A man named Florus agreed with Augustine, but the reaction of some was to say that if everything depended on God then they themselves should not be rebuked for anything they did. 'Why is it my fault,' they asked, 'if I don't have what I have not received from Him, when He alone can give it?'

At Augustine's suggestion Florus paid a visit to Hippo and after talking with him Augustine sent back another substantial booklet entitled *Rebuke and Grace*, in which he rebuked them for not wanting to be rebuked and declared that apart from the grace of God 'men do absolutely no good thing in thought, word or action'. He also asserted that the number of the predestined was fixed before the world began, 'neither to be increased nor diminished', but added that no one could be sure he was one of the elect so long as he was alive, since it was always possible that he had not been granted the gift of perseverance. 'To some of His own children whom He has regenerated in Christ, to whom He has given faith, hope and love, God does not give perseverance also. If I am asked why God should not have given them perseverance, I answer that I do not know. Let them with us condescend to be ignorant, without a murmur against God.'

Failure to persevere would prove that, after all, the person was not one of the elect, and 'those who do not belong to that most certain and blessed number are most righteously judged according to their deservings'. When confronted with Paul's statement that God 'wants all men to be saved' (1 Timothy 2 :4), he declared that by analogy with the use of the word in other New Testament passages 'all' meant 'all the pre-destined'. He denied that the verse could possibly mean that people are not saved simply because they are unwilling to believe. It is 'not because *they* do not will it but because God does not', for he regarded it as beyond question that God 'did not will to do anything that He has not done'.

Before long this restatement of his convictions began to cause misgivings, this time in the south of France. A youth named Hilary, who had formerly lived at Hippo, wrote to Augustine in 428, sending greetings from his parents but explaining that many people in Marseilles were disturbed by 'this new theory' which seemed to make preaching useless. They could not accept the idea that the number of the elect had already been fixed, as to some extent the issue must depend on the use each man made of the free will God had given him. Augustine's words made people despair. 'I ought not to refrain from telling you,' Hilary was quick to add, 'that they profess to admire your Holiness in all your words and deeds, with this exception.' Conscious of his immaturity and admitting that 'all of us are weary of it', Hilary arranged for a theologian named Prosper to write at the same time.

'Many of the servants of Christ who live in the city of Marseilles,' explained Prosper, 'think that your argument on the calling of the elect according to the design of God is con-trary to the opinion of the Fathers and the tradition of the Church.' Prosper regretted that he himself was no match for them and 'their most evil belief', since they included the gifted young bishop of Arles, 'an admirer of your teaching in all other matters'. The objectors asserted that 'the blood of Christ was offered for all men without exception, hence all who are willing to approach to faith and baptism can be saved'. To say that the question of personal salvation or damnation had already been settled 'according to the pleasure of the Creator' would undermine all effort, since 'the outcome cannot be other than what God has determined and under the name of predestination a certain inevitability of fate is introduced'. In their view 'Our Lord Jesus Christ died for the whole human race : as far as God is concerned, eternal life is prepared for all; but as far as the freedom of the will is concerned, eternal life is won by those who believe by their own choice.'

Augustine replied to Hilary and Prosper in *The Predestination of the Saints* and *The Gift of Perseverance*, written when he was rising seventy-five. These books reveal no weakening in his powers of thought and expression, though they do go over the same ground again and again. To his critics he yielded not one inch. He admitted that earlier in life 'I was in a similar error, thinking that the faith whereby we believe in God is in us from ourselves and that by it we obtain the gifts of God', but he had been compelled to change his mind, mainly by Paul's words, 'What do you have that you did not receive?' (1 Corinthians 4 : 7). He therefore re-affirmed his conviction that 'grace precedes faith', so that believers have 'received from the Father the gift by which to believe in Christ', the difference between them and unbelievers being that 'to the former it is given to believe, to the latter it is not given'. Only those whom God has predestined to be His children become believers. 'Predestination is the preparation for grace; grace is the donation itself.' Tirelessly he drummed it into his readers that 'God elected believers : He chose them that they might be so, not because they already were so.' Men do not believe in order to be numbered with the elect : they are 'elected to believe', and he cited the opening chapter of the Epistle to the Ephesians — 'a trumpet of truth so clear' — to prove his point.

He flatly denied the Pelagian suggestion that God predestined Christians to be His children because he foresaw that they would believe. No, it was 'not because we were to be so, but that we might be so'. Asked why God did not teach everyone to believe, he replied, 'As we speak justly when we say concerning any teacher of literature who is alone in a city, "He teaches literature here to everybody," not that all men learn but that there is none who learns literature who does not learn from him, so we justly say "God teaches all men to come to Christ", not because all come but because none comes in any other way.'

The longer he went on the more inflexible he became. New epigrams crowded into his mind as he dictated. 'Let him who is delivered love His grace; let him who is not delivered acknowledge his due.' 'He who is delivered has good grounds for thankfulness; he who is condemned has no ground for finding fault.' With his uncanny ability to draw Scripture verses to his aid, he confronted critics of God's fairness with the householder's answers to his indignant employees in Christ's parable of the labourers in the vineyard, 'Take what belongs to you, and go. I choose to give to this last as I give to you. Am I not allowed to do what I choose with what belongs to me? Or do you begrudge my generosity?' (Matthew 20:14–15). Asked why one person should be punished by God and another delivered, he replied, 'I can find no answer; as His anger is righteous and His mercy great, so His judgments are unsearchable.' In support of all this he could only say, 'God's books lie open, let us not turn away our view: the divine Scripture cries aloud, let us give it a hearing.'

He did not shirk the problem posed by Christ's admission that the inhabitants of Tyre and Sidon would have repented if they had witnessed the deeds He did in other places. 'Although he foresaw that they would believe His miracles if they should be done among them, He willed not to come to their help since in His predestination—secret indeed but yet righteous—He had determined otherwise concerning them.' Since God had not predestined them to be believers, even the opportunity of faith was denied them. It was just the same with unbaptised infants. 'Often when the parents are eager and the ministers prepared for giving baptism, it is still not given.' Why not? Because God had not elected those children before the foundation of the world to be Christians. So what happens to them? 'Not being regenerated, they pass into the second death and the wrath of God abides on them.' To those who were shocked at this conclusion his reply was, 'Again and again we say "Who are you, a man, to answer back to God?"' (Romans 9 : 20).

In thus leaving no loophole for compassion, Augustine claimed to be rightly interpreting the New Testament and he could point to anticipations of this emphasis in his own earlier writings, as well as in those of Ambrose and others. He felt that what he was saying had always formed part of the faith of the Church and was implicit in her prayers when she asked God to move people to repentance. In his opinion he was not teaching something new but re-emphasising old truth to meet the need of his time. 'Let those who think I am in error consider again and again, carefully, what is said here, lest perchance they themselves may be mistaken.'

He saw no reason why belief in predestination should inhibit preaching, any more than it did in Paul's case. In fact he urged that predestination must be preached, even if some misunderstood it like the man who deserted the monastery at Hippo after saying, 'Whatever I may be now, I shall be what God has foreknown I shall be.'

Augustine did not explain the relationship between these doctrines and the cross of Christ. Although it might have been considered the cornerstone of his system, he never seems to have stated that Christ bore the sins only of those whom God had predestined to be forgiven. But he did suggest that Jesus Himself was the supreme example of predestination, in that His human nature was taken up 'by God into the Son of God' by pure grace, having done nothing to merit this.

Chapter Thirty-Six

THE VANDALS ARE COMING

Augustine longed to speak again to Count Boniface, but he was afraid his postman might not survive to deliver the letter and that then it might fall into the wrong hands. Eventually he found a thoroughly reliable man whom he had reason to believe would be able to get into the general's presence. He wrote very carefully but boldly, alluding to many evils which he attributed to Boniface himself, 'associated as you are with multitudes of armed men whose passions must be humoured and whose cruelty is dreaded'. It was a delicate task bringing the excesses of his troops to the notice of their commander. 'So complete has been the havoc wrought in order to indulge their passions that it would be difficult now to find anything for the plunderer to carry away.' Indeed by this time Numidia was sinking into chaos as the mountain barriers on its southern rim were repeatedly breached.

'What shall I say of the devastation of Africa by hordes of African barbarians, to whom no resistance is offered, while you are engrossed with such embarrassments in your own circumstances that you are taking no measures for averting this calamity? Who would have believed, after Boniface had become a Count of the Empire and been placed in command in Africa with so large an army and such great authority, that the same man who formerly as Tribune kept all these barbarous tribes in peace by storming their strongholds and menacing them with his small band of brave confederates, should now have suffered the barbarians to be so bold, to encroach so far, to destroy and plunder so much, to turn into deserts such vast regions once densely peopled? Where were any found who did not predict that, as soon as you obtained the authority of Count, the African hordes would not only be checked but made tributaries to the Roman Empire? And now you yourself perceive how completely the event has disappointed men's hopes.'

Augustine was aware that as Boniface read these words at his headquarters he would feel indignant that he, who had been so grievously deceived and harrassed by his own side, should be blamed for the country's calamities. He imagined the Count turning on him and asking, 'In circumstances so difficult, what do you want me to do?' Not being trained for politics or war, Augustine could only approach him at a personal level, quoting such texts as 'Do not love the world or anything in the world' (1 John 2 : 15). He called upon the general to repent, to give alms, to pray and to fast. Then he went further :

'If you did not now have a wife, I would say to you what we said at Tubunae, that you should live in the holy state of continence, and would add that you should now do what we prevented you from doing at that time, namely withdraw yourself from the labours of military service so far as might be possible without prejudice to the public welfare. I am, however, prevented from exhorting you to that mode of life by your having a wife, since without her consent it is not lawful for you to live under a vow of continence, because— though you did wrong in marrying again after the declaration which you made at Tubunae—she, not being aware of this, became your wife innocently and without restrictions. Would that you could persuade her to agree to a vow of continence so that you might without hindrance render to God what you know to be due to Him. If, however, you cannot make this agreement with her, by all means guard carefully conjugal chastity and pray to God, who will deliver you out of your difficulties that you may at some future time be able to do what is meanwhile impossible. This does not affect your obligation to love God and not to love the world, to hold the faith steadfastly even in the cares of war—if you must still be engaged in them—and to seek peace. In all these duties your wife is not, or ought not to be, a hindrance to you.'

It was the best the old bishop could do, but it was not good enough. Read in camp by the man of war, surrounded by indisciplined soldiers and officers, tormented by tribal raids from the south and by punitive expeditions sent against him from Italy, as uncertain still of Rome's support for him as of his own loyalty to Rome, it failed to show him any meaningful way out of his dilemmas. He needed greater military power to survive. So on some dark day he invited the Vandals to cross over from Spain and help him.

History turned upon this fateful decision. In southern Spain the Vandals, after their long march from eastern Europe, had acquired a young commander named Gaiseric (or Genseric), a greater leader of men than Boniface or any general Rome could put in the field for the next fifty years. The Count's treacherous invitation, which he soon regretted, gave Gaiseric his chance. In May 429 he assembled his people on the beaches of Andalusia, eighty thousand of them. It was not far to Africa from there, eight miles at the nearest point, for the hills on either side of the Straits of Gibraltar stand in full view of one another. So they crossed over into Mauretania.

Hippo lay a thousand miles east of their bridgehead and the whole coast was a maze of mountains, cut from north to south by innumerable rivers flowing off the Atlas ranges, abounding in good defensive positions. But the countryside was seething with discontent and fear, for the great days of Roman military might had passed away. Vandal morale was high and Gaiseric was determined. At unbelievable speed the invaders moved eastwards. Possidius recorded their advance as refugees began to arrive in Hippo with their tales of woe. 'And now, the divine will permitting, there appeared in a short time great forces of the Vandal army with whom were associated Alans, Goths and people of other races, all armed with spears and exercised in war. They crossed the sea in ships from Spain and, pouring into Africa, spread over the land, penetrating into every part of Mauretania and even into our province and district. They perpetrated all the cruelties and atrocities imaginable : robbery, murder, torturings, burnings and innumerable other barbarities, so that the country became depopulated. They respected neither age nor sex, nor priest, nor ministers of God, nor church buildings. Marauding and destroying came these ferocious hordes.' He was not exaggerating. Even the English language retains the word 'vandal' to this day.

Some Christian ministers living in the path of the invasion asked Augustine's advice whether or not to evacuate. Though reluctant to forbid anyone to move to what appeared to be safer places, he reminded them that it was their duty to stand by the churches they were called to serve, and he quoted verses in the Psalms which speak of God as a defence and a strong tower. But bishop Honoratus of Mauretania objected. Referring to Christ's words, 'When you are persecuted in one place, flee to another' (Matthew 10 : 23), he pointed out that Mary and Joseph got away into Egypt from Herod and that Paul escaped over the wall of Damascus in a basket. 'I do not see what good we can do to ourselves or to the people by continuing to remain in the churches,' he wrote, 'except to see before our eyes men slain, women outraged, churches burned and ourselves expiring amid torments applied in order to extort from us what we do not possess.'

Augustine, who had had no personal experience of the horrors of war, was compelled to think again. He suggested that when a Christian leader became a marked man, as Paul was at Damascus, it was legitimate to leave, but when the whole community was in equal danger they should either evacuate together or the clergy should stay with the people. Alluding to Christ's words about the hireling who flees when he sees the wolf coming, he reminded Honoratus that 'God is powerful to hear the prayers of His children and to avert those things which they fear,' without realising that for the moment it was easier to say that in Numidia than in Mauretania. 'When dangers have reached their extremity,' he continued, 'and there is no possibility of escape by flight, an extraordinary crowd of persons of both sexes and all ages is wont to assemble in the church, some urgently asking for baptism, others for reconciliation, and all calling for consolation and strengthening through the administration of the sacraments. If the ministers be not at their posts at such a time, how great perdition overtakes those who depart from this life either not regenerated or not loosed from their sins. But if the ministers be at their posts through the strength which God bestows upon them, all are aided, some are baptised, others reconciled to the church. None are defrauded of the communion of the Lord's body; all are consoled, edified, and exhorted to ask God, who is able to do so, to avert all things which are feared, prepared for both alternatives.'

Envisaging the possibility that all the clergy could be wiped out, Augustine suggested that it might become right to cast lots to determine who should risk staying and who should make sure he escaped. 'In difficulties of this kind, God judges better than men.'

Chapter Thirty-Seven

JULIAN AND THE EXTREMIST

There was still a little time. Augustine's industrious secretaries were making copies of *The Mirror* which he had recently written, one of several books not destined to survive. It was an anthology of Old and New Testament texts drawn up for simple people to show what was commanded and what was forbidden, with a preface by the bishop. Possidius thought it rather good, saying, 'He who reads this volume will come to understand whether he lives in obedience or disobedience to God.'

In 429, hoping to effect a reconciliation with Boniface, Placidia sent to Africa a man named Darius, who not only succeeded in detaching the Count from his alliance with the Vandals but even persuaded the invaders themselves to agree to a truce. He did not visit Hippo, so Augustine never met him, as 'my bodily weakness and the chill of age' ruled out the long journey to Carthage. Hearing a friend's favourable impression of Darius, Augustine wrote to thank him for having 'stayed war itself with a word', applying to him the saying of Christ, 'Blessed are the peacemakers, for they will be called sons of God.' (Matthews 5 :9).

Darius was so pleased to hear from the old man that he replied enthusiastically, sending Augustine medicines and money for the repair of his books, asking in return for a copy of the *Confessions*. Encouraged to get a friendly letter from such a distinguished man, Augustine answered with equal warmth, 'I was delighted with your letter, exceedingly delighted.' Darius' wife had recently presented him with a son, but this time the bishop made no attempt to counsel his correspondent on domestic matters. Instead he quoted

Horace and several other poets before alluding to 'the great Teacher' and the Apostle Paul. In his eagerness he sent five books as well as the *Confessions*, adding to the latter his own excellent advice : 'In these behold me, that you may not praise me beyond what I am; in these believe what is said of me not by others but by myself; in these contemplate me and see what I have been in myself, by myself; and if anything in me please you, join me in praising Him to whom, and not to myself, I desire praise to be given.'

Turning seventy-six towards the end of the year, he found he had reached the point at which one no longer wants to go anywhere. 'I might have come if it had not been winter,' he wrote in declining an invitation to the dedication of a church, 'I might have braved the winter if I had been young.' He had plenty to do without moving more than a few yards. On his desk lay a copy of Julian's reply to the book he had published against him. As was his custom, he first gave time to mastering its contents.

About nine years had passed since the start of their heated argument, but Julian was still tormented by Augustine's insistence that infants needed to be baptised if they were not to be justly condemned to an eternity in hell because of the infection of sin derived from Adam. 'If there is no sin without the will,' he objected, 'if no will where freedom has not developed, if no freedom where there is no faculty of choice based on the use of reason, by what fearful miracle is sin found in babies who do not possess the use of reason and consequently lack the faculty of choice and hence have no will and therefore, by an irrefutable chain of argument, no sin whatever?'

From this basic contention Julian, who was almost as competent a master of rhetoric as Augustine himself, launched a furious attack upon the inner citadel of the bishop's faith. 'Who was it,' he demanded, 'who declared the innocent guilty, who was so heartless, so harsh, so oblivious of God and justice, who was so barbaric a tyrant, deserving the hatred of the human race, by failing to spare not only those who had not sinned but even those who were incapable of sinning? Who is this person who punishes the innocent? When you answer "God" you give us a real shock. We can scarcely believe such terrible sacrilege. We are uncertain what you mean. We know that the word can be used in various senses, "as indeed there are many 'gods' and many 'lords', yet for us there is but one God, the Father, from whom all things came, and but one Lord, Jesus Christ, through whom we live." (1 Corinthians 8 :5–6). Which god, then, are you accusing? At this point, most reverend bishop, you give vent to something sadder and more horrible than the pit of Avernus exhales. The same God, you say, who commends His love towards us, who loved us and did not spare His own Son but gave Him up for us, He it is who passes this verdict, who persecutes newborn babies and assigns infants to eternal flames, infants whom He knows are incapable of either good or evil. What a cruel, blasphemous, pernicious belief! You have departed so far from piety, from culture, even from plain common sense, as to believe that your God is guilty of injustice. How much more tolerable it would be to abandon the profession of religion altogether than to follow its course through such perilous territory.' He went on to upbraid Augustine for his sheer stupidity and to lampoon as a monstrous fabrication the idea that God managed the creation of mankind so badly that by one wicked act Adam threw away all his natural good qualities and 'only sin and the necessity of sinning clung inseparably to him'.

So in his old age Augustine, who in youth had dared to cross swords with Jerome, was himself confronted not only by the Vandals on the borders of Numidia but with an angry young man challenging his mature convictions and ridiculing him in public. He could not do much about the Vandals but he refused to let Julian go unanswered. Line for line, blow for blow, he retaliated, dictating far into the spring nights, refusing to modify his position in any way, for 'it was not I who devised original sin'. The Scriptures were open before him under the lamp : 'By one man's disobedience many were made sinners' (Romans : 5 : 19), 'Who are you, a man, to answer back to God?' (Romans 9 : 20), 'Whoever believes and is baptised will be saved' (Mark 16 : 16), 'I tell you the truth, unless a man is born of water and the Spirit, he cannot enter the kingdom of God' (John 3 : 5), and many more which his fertile brain produced in abundance and marshalled with extraordinary skill. He was determined not to compromise, not to allow Julian to defeat him, not to exchange God's word for human sentiment.

Temperamentally he was an extremist. Time and again he had pushed truth to its limits and beyond, sometimes echoing the common assumptions of his age but always by his innate genius imparting authority to what he advocated. It was one thing to turn away from moral indiscipline and promiscuity, but quite another to despise marriage as inferior to celibacy and expect married couples to limit their sexual intercourse to the minimum necessary for having children. It was one thing to rejoice in the fellowship of Christian believers throughout the Empire, but quite another to deny salvation to anyone not in his own Church and call in the state to suppress them as criminals. It was one thing to proclaim that the love of God is shed abroad in our hearts by the Holy Spirit, but quite another to regard cruel persecution to compel men to join the Catholic Church as a legitimate expression of that love. It was one thing to trace human perversity to its source in the fall of the first man, but quite another to assert that infants who died unbaptised were rightly assigned to eternal damnation. It was one thing to teach that Christians ought to be baptised, but quite another to invest the rite itself with automatically regenerating effect, so that all those baptised in his Church, and only those, were saved. It was one thing to urge Christians to acknowledge that it was not really they who chose Christ but Christ who chose them, but quite another to attribute salvation so exclusively to God's grace that damnation was due to God withholding His grace. It was one thing to maintain that the omniscient God knew before the creation of the world who would believe in Christ and who would not, but quite another to assert that He had already fixed the destiny of all mankind by irrevocably assigning a minority to eternal bliss and the majority to eternal torment, and that with perfect justice. It was one thing to believe that God still works miraculously in the lives of men and women, but quite another to encourage a superstitious cult of the supposed relics of martyrs. In all these cases Augustine adopted the extreme position, denigrating those who disagreed with him, his character and reputation ensuring that most of his views prevailed in Christendom for a thousand years and that all are influential to this day.

Chapter Thirty-Eight

THE VOICE FROM THE SILENT CITY

During the truce Augustine continued preaching to the anxious people of Hippo, his congregations swollen by those who had fled from their homes farther west. 'Have you given all you had to the barbarians, brother?' he asked them one day. 'I gave the whole lot,' was the reply he suggested, 'I was left naked, but I stayed alive.' 'Why did you do that?' the bishop went on. 'I was going to be killed, that was why I gave everything.' The experience had been only too common and Augustine made the most of it. 'Why was it that this happened to you? Shall I tell you? Because before the barbarians arrived on the scene you never helped the poor, so that through the poor your alms might reach Christ. To Christ you gave not a whit; to the barbarians you gave all you had. Christ asks, and receives nothing; the barbarian tortures, and carries off everything. If you have redeemed your life at such a price, how great a price must be paid for eternal life? You give to the enemy so that you may go on living as a beggar. Give something to Christ so that you may live on in blessedness. You still have something. You have yourself. It is from the devil that you need to be redeemed, the devil who drags you with him to the second death, the eternal fire. To redeem yourself from the second death you need righteousness. The barbarian could first take your money from you and then keep you captive, so that you would have no means of redeeming yourself once all your property was in the hands of the man who had you in his hands too. But righteousness is something you do not lose against your will. It abides in the inmost treasure house of the heart. Hold it fast, make it your own and you will be

redeemed from the second death. Christ went through afflic-
tion, abuse, false accusations, spitting in the face, through a
crown of thorns, through the cross, through death. Why do
you remain sitting still? Shame on you, you full-grown man,
shame on you! Women have followed Him. Your Lord, our
Lord, their Lord, the Redeemer of our life, by pioneering a
rough and narrow path has made it a roadway for you, a safe
and well paved road.'

But not even the diplomacy of Darius could halt the Vandals for long. In the spring of 430 they surged forwards again,
cutting eastwards through the mountains of Numidia. The
only place they failed to take was Cirta, perched on its lofty
crag where today the road tunnels several times through a
precipice to reach the summit. They bypassed it, leaving the
forlorn defenders to gaze desperately at the surrounding hills
from which no relief was ever to come. Cut off from retreat
to his base at Carthage, Count Boniface withdrew the rem-
nants of his mercenary army to the coast at Hippo. So the
Vandals went on to besiege the capital, whose large population and guardian lake kept them at bay. These were the
only three Roman cities to survive the summer onslaught.

For the time being Hippo was safe, protected by its mountain, rivers, swamps and lofty ridges, with Boniface's men
on guard and the sea lanes open to Italy. Refugees poured
in as the surrounding countryside was overrun. Happily
Possidius escaped from Calama in time to join Augustine, for
he was the only man on either side to leave any account of
what happened. Other bishops who had lost everything came
in, but Possidius regretted 'it was not possible to supply them
with all the things they needed'. On the plain outside Hippo
and up in the hills, all the towns were burnt and the population decimated, 'given over to torture, slain by the sword,
sold into captivity'. Others got away to hide in woods and
rocky mountains, where death from starvation soon stared
them in the face. In Hippo they had first-hand evidence of
the magnitude of the disaster. Nothing was hidden from

Augustine. 'Tears were his bread day and night. They were mournful and bitter beyond all others because of his old age and because life was now nearing its end. We remember that whilst sitting together and conversing at table Augustine said to us, "You must know that in this time of calamity I have prayed to God that He might deliver this city and, if this was not His holy will, that He would give strength to His servants to submit to His decrees, and also that He might be pleased to take me to Himself out of this world." And saying this whilst we listened, each and every one of us who were in the city with him prayed together to the good God.'

During the first three months of the siege of Hippo, Augustine went on with his usual work of preaching and writing. 'He was sound in all the members of his body and enjoyed good sight and hearing,' Possidius recorded, though Augustine himself might have put it differently. 'As you can see,' he said in one of his last sermons, 'in years I have only recently become an old man, but in physical weakness I have long been old. But I shall not desert you. Pray for me that I may serve you in the word of God as long as there is life in this body.'

In the great heat of August he was forced to take to his bed, exhausted by fever. He ceased dictating several books on which he was still working, including his reply to Julian, which has since become known as *The Unfinished Work*, for 'this, as it happened, was his last illness, nor did the Lord withhold from His servant what he sought in his prayers'. As he lay there, white-haired in the doomed city, an invalid came to be healed. 'If I possessed any such gift of healing,' said Augustine, 'don't you think I would use it in my own case first?' However, when the man explained that God had told him in a dream to go to the bishop, he relented and laid hands on him.

Then he asked his companions to write out the seven so-called Penitential Psalms—Psalms 6, 32, 38, 51, 102, 130 and 143—and hang them up on the wall of his room so that he could see them as he lay in bed. 'He recited them continuously and whilst he did this he shed bitter and abundant tears.' He wanted to end his life in humility, remembering how great a sinner he had been. He did not weep because he was afraid to die, for 'with Christ death is not to be feared', nor had he any doubts about what lay beyond it. 'When the final judgment has been completed there will be two kingdoms, the one Christ's, the other the devil's, the one consisting of the good, the other of the bad. The former will live happily in eternal life. The reward of virtue will be God Himself : we shall see Him for ever, we shall love Him without satiety, we shall praise Him without weariness. After all God's works, He rested on the seventh day and the voice of His book tells us that after our works we also will rest with Him in the sabbath of everlasting life. The seventh day is without evening : it has no sunset.'

Repentant and trusting in 'the Mediator, through whom we climb from the depths to the heights', he lay there for a few weeks, remembering. 'And lest his reflections might be disturbed by anyone during the ten days before he died, he asked to be left alone and that no one would enter his room except when the doctor came to see him or his food was being brought. We observed his wishes and did not disturb him. He spent all the time in prayer.' So at the last he did attain that total separation from earthly distractions which had beckoned him ever since the months at Cassiciacum. And then, on August 28, 430 'while we stood around him, watching him and joining him in prayer, he sank into sleep with his fathers. And for his eternal repose on the day of his burial the holy sacrifice was offered up, at which we were all present. He made no will, for as a poor man of God he had no possessions.' Soon afterwards Possidius, the first and most important of Augustine's many biographers, set down the main facts not already made public in the *Confessions* about 'that great man with whom I lived for nearly forty years in the closest friendship and in all sweetness, without trouble or disagreement'. He felt that those who had actually seen Augustine, listened to him and been intimate with him had benefitted from his life beyond all others, although in his numerous books 'it can be seen how, with God's help, Augustine became so great in the Church and in these works the faithful shall find that Augustine lives for ever.'

The storm of the world went on. After the siege had lasted another eleven months, Boniface evacuated Hippo and the Vandals burnt it. Four years later Carthage fell to them and Gaiseric became master of the central Mediterranean, even in his turn sacking Rome. For a hundred years the Vandals prevailed, dealing rigorously with all who were not Arians, particularly the Catholic Church, whose buildings were confiscated and clergy expelled. But Roman power survived in Constantinople and when eventually North Africa was recaptured the Vandals lost their racial identity and disappeared. The most decisive conquest of all took place another hundred years later when the Arabs poured in from the East. They brought with them their language and a new religion, Islam. Before long both Punic and Latin fell into disuse, though the original Berber languages continued to be spoken in the mountains. Arabic became dominant and has remained so till this day.

But it was not only Roman rule and the Latin tongue which deserted that splendid coast. Hippo itself was abandoned. In time earth covered the old town; crops were planted, goats grazed, and houses were built over it. For a thousand years it was a lost city. Not until 1924, during the period of French rule in Algeria, was it excavated and men gazed in amazement at the skeleton of Augustine's church and walked the massive paving stones he knew so well. Then the French left, as the Romans had left, and the site began to silt up once more. Trees, weeds and goats have returned, while the roads and factories of the sprawling town of Annaba threaten to engulf the silent city.

And in the centuries that followed the coming of the Arabs, Christianity itself disappeared from North Africa. All those churches, all those Catholics, Donatists and Arians became as though they had never been. The Church sank into the grave of the Empire and Islam took over. The failure of Augustine and his contemporaries to move the gospel out of its Roman framework into a Berber context proved fatal. In the end Christianity was left with only romantic ruins, broken masonry, fallen pillars and the books that were written there, especially the books of Augustine, thanks to which it is still true, as it was in his lifetime, that 'the bishop is speaking'.

ROMAN EMPERORS IN THE WEST
DURING THE ADULT LIFE OF AUGUSTINE

VALENTINIAN I	364–375
born 321	
GRATIAN	375–383
born 359	
Maximus (usurper)	383–388
VALENTINIAN II	375–392
born 371	
Eugenius (usurper)	392–394
THEODOSIUS	394–395
born 346	
HONORIUS	395–423
born 384	
John (usurper)	423–425
VALENTINIAN III	425–455
born 419	

INDEX OF QUOTATIONS
FROM THE BIBLE

The wording of most of these quotations has been made to conform to that of the New International Version or the Revised Standard Version.

INDEX OF AUGUSTINE'S BOOKS

All the books by Augustine listed below are mentioned in this biography. Some of the titles vary in different English translations. There are also many quotations from other books he wrote, as well as from his letters and sermons.

INDEX OF QUOTATIONS

Unless otherwise indicated, all quotations are from the works of Augustine. In some cases these have been frequently translated so that there are several different English versions.

GENERAL INDEX

The following names, which occur frequently, are not included in this index: Africa, Augustine, Carthage, Catholic Church, Hippo, Italy, Numidia, Roman Empire, Rome.